SPEAKING OF
POLITICS

*Preparing College Students for Democratic
Citizenship through Deliberative Dialogue*

Dedicated to the memory of our mothers

Jean K. Harriger (1921-2005)
who liked to talk, but knew how to listen

and

Mary Elizabeth Hall Jordan (1914-1949)
whose example as a young teacher of
"expression" inspired me many
years later to take up her cause with
a new generation of young people

Acknowledgments

Without the 30 young people, the Democracy Fellows, who began this journey with us—and especially the 26 who completed it—there would be no book, and more important, no long-term look at how extensive exposure to deliberative democracy can affect college students. Because these students were promised anonymity from the start, we cannot list their names here, but we express to them our profound gratitude and readily acknowledge that in the pages of this book, what the reader will hear is in large part their story, not ours. Likewise, we thank the members of the cohort group who offered their time each year and their voices to provide us a counterbalance to the experiences and expressions of the Democracy Fellows, and the deliberation participants—those one-time deliberators from the fall of 2002—who taught us one of this study's most profound lessons: that even a single experience with deliberation can indeed alter one's political outlook and optimism.

In every project of this magnitude and length, there are individuals who step up to help in invaluable ways, and that was our experience as well: from the Wake Forest administration, Ross Griffith of the Office of Institutional Records regularly provided us with timely statistical information and advice and assistance about how to use it, and Ken Zick and Mary Gerardy, from our Division of Student Life, also lent feedback and encouragement. Undergraduate and graduate student assistants performed vital tasks: Nicole Kazee and Allison Crawford did critical background research; Rebecca Jerome and Terry Dumansky scheduled and managed the paper work on interviews and focus groups; Elizabeth Lundeen did virtually everything mentioned here, but her most notable and unique contributions were her exemplary copyediting and footnote/citation management; Terry Dumansky and Colleen Colaner helped with thematic analyses of certain data sets; and Leanne Quatrucci, Allison Spangler, and Connie Chesner assisted in the assembling of annual reports. Joanne Vansice served this project with transcription par excellance. Her skill, professionalism, and abiding good humor through garbled tapes and all manner of other human and technologically induced errors was remarkable.

Underpinning all of the on-site help was the continual presence and support of John Dedrick of the Kettering Foundation. Though keeping us grounded and realistic from the start was not an easy task, John managed to do that in his own kind and inimitable way. We also are grateful for the gentle presence and support of Debi Witte and, later in the project, Laura Grattan. Ilse Tebbetts proved to be an effective and accommodating editor as she assisted us in our attempt to give this story its best hearing.

Finally, we thank Bob Griffiths and Toney McMillan, our husbands and partners, and our respective families for their patience and support during this lengthy project.

Contents

Foreword

An Experiment of More Than Ordinary Significance

S peaking of Politics is about a discovery and an invention—a breakthrough in combating the privatization that threatens to rob college students of their public lives. This is also a book about faculty members Katy Harriger and Jill McMillan, who went beyond charted waters to combat this threat. And it is a book that challenges colleges and universities to take more seriously their mission statements to prepare students to be citizens.

The argument that preparing students to be citizens requires the same self-conscious effort as preparing them to be historians, musicians, or accountants can be very unsettling. For instance, a faculty member at another institution reported that when he pressed for specifics on what his institution was doing to provide the civic education promised in the catalog, he was met with considerable resistance. The issue didn't resonate well with most of his colleagues, and they quickly tired of his persistence in raising it. They found a solution: they took the reference to citizenship out of the catalog.

This incident is relevant here because Wake Forest hasn't abandoned its responsibility for civic education. In fact, the two faculty members who wrote this book have given a new meaning to this type of education by giving a new meaning to democratic politics. That was the invention that led to a breakthrough. Students in the experiment discovered another dimension to democracy and a new role for themselves as citizens. The effect of what happened at Wake Forest was so profound that the Kettering Foundation has touted the Democracy Fellows project as one of the most significant innovations it has seen in 20 years. (Kettering's relation to the experiment, I should explain, has been that of a research institution, which doesn't make grants.) What happened at Wake Forest happened because two members of the faculty had compelling reasons to change how they went about their work as teachers and scholars.

The Wake Forest experiment is significant because it was informed by an acute sense of the troubles facing modern democracy. Professors Harriger and McMillan have been very aware of the contest now going on over the kind of democracy that will shape the twenty-first century and the role citizens will play in it. The democracy that characterized the second half of the twentieth century is in serious trouble. Look at the titles of several recent books: *Demosclerosis*, *Democracy's Discontent*, *Democracy at Risk*, *Downsizing Democracy*.[1] All of these studies report that democracy is facing fundamental problems, which I have called "megachallenges." Determining where higher education stands in all this ferment seems inescapable to me. And the Wake Forest experiment addresses one of the most serious of these challenges—the relegation of the supposedly sovereign citizenry to the sidelines of politics.

Americans sense that they have been marginalized, and in one of the books just cited, Matthew Crenson and Benjamin Ginsberg show why. "For more than two centuries," they write, "ordinary citizens were important actors," but they argue that our political system has found ways to operate without a collective public.[2] People sense their marginalization and see evidence of it in gerrymandered districts that discount the votes of all but the core of electors needed to return most incumbents to office. And while citizens like to hear the government promise to be more responsive to them as customers, they know that they should *own* the store. In Kettering's most recent research on how Americans feel

---

[1] Jonathan Rauch, *Demosclerosis: The Silent Killer of American Government* (New York: Random House, 1994); Michael J. Sandel, *Democracy's Discontent: America in Search of a Public Philosophy* (Cambridge, MA: Belknap Press of Harvard University Press, 1996); Stephen Macedo et al., *Democracy at Risk: How Political Choices Undermine Citizen Participation and What We Can Do about It* (Washington, DC: Brookings Institution Press, 2005); and Matthew A. Crenson and Benjamin Ginsberg, *Downsizing Democracy: How America Sidelined Its Citizens and Privatized Its Public* (Baltimore, MD: Johns Hopkins University Press, 2002).

[2] Crenson and Ginsberg, *Downsizing Democracy*, p. ix.

about the country's political system, one refrain stands out. People say over and over, "we can't make a difference." [3]

Crenson and Ginsberg lay much of the blame for this situation on the advent of a "personal democracy" that encourages citizens to pursue their individual interests or assert their individual rights, much as consumers would. This encouragement reduces incentives for people to work together. The two scholars cite some of the community service programs now popular at schools and colleges across the country as examples of how personal democracy has changed civic education. Individuals volunteering to serve others is admirable, yet it is different from joint efforts to correct the conditions that require volunteering. Though not unsympathetic to service learning, Crenson and Ginsberg come to the same conclusion as Harriger and McMillan—it has become an alternative to politics and isn't training for sovereignty.

For some time, college students have had the impression that their institutions aren't concerned about citizens being sidelined. In 1993, a Kettering study found that undergraduates thought all academe had to offer was a curriculum in political science for those interested in the subject.[4] This arrangement fit comfortably with students' perception that politics is for people who intend to serve as politicians or to work in government, careers that had limited appeal. Now, 14 years later, this book reports that many students still believe their institutions are better at preparing them for a career than for an active life in a democracy.

The idea that there is a political dimension to life doesn't appear to have crossed the minds of most undergraduates. This is telling. Political theorists have argued that the tragedy of the modern world is that "politics," the work of politicians and governments,

---

[3] Doble Research Associates, *Public Thinking about Democracy's Challenge: Reclaiming the Public's Role, An Analysis of Results from the 2005-2006 National Issues Forums* (Dayton, OH: Kettering Foundation, 2006).

[4] The Harwood Group, *College Students Talk Politics* (Dayton, OH: Kettering Foundation, 1993).

so dominates the culture that we have lost an appreciation for "the political," the life we have with our fellow citizens, which isn't confined to what we do through governments. What students have said is confirmation of this domination. Undergraduates have little sense of themselves as actors in the larger political world.

As Kettering reported in 1993 (and as this book reports now), students have had largely negative feelings about politics. This alienation pushes them into their private lives where they feel they can make a difference with family and friends. The negative impressions of politics not only come from television but also come from campuses. Undergraduates in the Kettering study said that their campus culture was dominated by adversarial extremes and that they felt pressure to be more partisan. For example, a Wake Forest student complained, "People are very opinionated in my classes. There is no moderation at all and [the discussion] gets totally out of bounds."[5] These diatribes seem more likely to exacerbate rather than solve problems.

The most encouraging comments students made in the 1990s interviews came when they were pressed on what might be done to improve politics. They didn't talk primarily about making reforms through legislation and government action; they spoke more about changing the tenor of politics. Students didn't expect to hear less emotion, but they wanted less acrimony. They thought there should be more appreciation for the gray areas between polarized positions. And they wanted to know more about trade-offs and sacrifices that would have to be made if popular solutions were adopted. The study also found that undergraduates had difficulty talking about what politics should be like because they lacked a conceptual framework for democracy and a common language for talking about it. Nonetheless, students were deeply concerned about the problems of society and appeared to have an instinct for a more deliberative democracy.

[5] David Mathews, Preface to *College Students Talk Politics*, p. vii.

Recent studies suggest that students' attitudes toward electoral politics may be a bit more favorable. Volunteering also remains popular, and there has been some increase in interest in civic action and community politics.[6] Yet after reviewing the literature, Harriger and McMillan note that even with evidence of an upswing, "interest in politics and political engagement is still half of what it was for young people when freshmen surveys began in the 1960s."[7]

To counter this alienation and privatization, the Wake Forest project used a new strategy. The Democracy Fellows were introduced to the most basic form of democracy, one in which citizens acquire the power to make a difference by joining forces in collective efforts. To rule themselves, people obviously have to have the power to act. And the generation of that power is affected early on by the way decisions are made. Of course, there are many ways of making collective decisions, but not all of them generate the same intensity or political power and commitment. Collective enterprises can be launched by following the persuasive argument of a leader. And they can be cobbled together through negotiations among different factions. Political will is strongest, however, when it grows out of what people believe is essential for their well-being.

The difficulty with tapping into these primarily political motivations is that there are a number of them, and citizens differ on which should be given preference in specific circumstances. For instance, even though everyone wants to be safe from danger as well as free from coercion, there may be some situations when it might be prudent to trade a bit of security to protect our freedom and others when just the opposite is wise. Making sound judgments about what is most appropriate is crucial. So the first political act is making a collective decision when there is a discrepancy between what is happening to us and what we think *should* be happening,

---

[6] Higher Education Research Institute, *The American Freshman: National Norms for Fall 2005* (Los Angeles: UCLA, n.d.).

[7] For recent data, visit CIRCLE's Web site to learn more about youth volunteering trends. See http://www.civicyouth.org.

yet there is no agreement on what *should* be. The Democracy Fellows were introduced to politics by being challenged to make such difficult decisions, not only with their fellow students, but also with citizens in Winston-Salem, the town where the university is located.

Because there are no experts on questions of what should be, we have to determine whether a proposed course of action is consistent with what is truly valuable to us. And we do that by weighing various proposals for action against the things we think are most important. To weigh in this fashion reminded the ancients of the scale used to determine the value of goods in the village market (sometimes called a *forum*). One word for this scale was *līthrā* (literally "the stone used in weighing"). And so, making decisions in which things of value have to be considered and sound judgment is required has been called *deliberation*, a term derived from the word for "scale." (I also like the Greek description of this way of deciding, which is "the talk we use to teach ourselves before we act.")

Deliberation, when presented as part of action and not merely a different way for people to talk, opens a door into politics for students who say that they don't know how to get meaningfully involved. This door can be opened without pressure from a powerful lobby and without a large donation to an election campaign. All that's needed is an opinion about what should be happening and a willingness to consider the opinions of others. These provide the motivation for an exchange of views that leads to collective decisions needed for effective collective action.

Deliberation also opens the door into "the political." The Wake Forest students were introduced to a political world underneath the major institutions of government. They saw how a democracy engages its citizens, generates political will, informs judgment, and amasses the powers needed for effective action. At Kettering, we call this the "organic" form of democracy to distinguish it from institutional politics and the machinery of government. Organic democracy can't be measured by institutional standards: Networks are more important than scale, power is relational, not legal, and a shared sense of direction trumps a majority vote. The public is not simply a consensual body; it is a primary source of political energy.

As Wake Forest students worked to make decisions with other citizens on things that were dear to everyone, they may have had the first inkling that they were already in the political world. One of the graduates of the project, reflecting on the experience, said that it had affected nearly everything she did. Her testimony is an indication that she discovered the political dimension of her own life. When students have this insight—when they realize they can be political actors—they have had a truly liberal education, which is an education that is liberating.

As we read the results of the Wake Forest experiment at the foundation, we wanted to know how students who understood the larger world of politics thought about politics in the conventional sense. Significantly, the fellows were more, not less, likely to vote—even though they knew that the elections were not the be-all and end-all of democracy. And unlike the students not in the experiment, who thought of citizenship primarily as asserting individual rights, the fellows seemed more inclined to think of citizenship in terms of responsibilities carried out through collective problem solving. And they may have distinguished between service *to* others and collective work *with* others. Certainly the graduates of the Democracy Fellows program weren't prone to be just consumers of government services. Hopefully, they will carry a robust, strong understanding of democracy into the twenty-first century.

The Wake Forest experiment not only has implications for college students and preparation for life as citizens but also has implications for the university itself and all of higher education. At Wake Forest, it should be worth noting that while the fellows became more critical of the political system (perhaps because they were more aware of what it could be), they were more likely to commend the institution for preparing them for citizenship— and more likely to feel that their voices were heard on campus (perhaps because they had learned how to create a public voice).

Equally significant, this report doesn't show that one group of Wake Forest students received a civic education and another didn't. All of the students received an education in politics while on campus—but the politics they learned was quite different. The implication for all of higher education is obvious. Every institution influences the way its students understand the political system and their role in it, whether or not the institution intends to. The question is, are colleges and universities content with what their students learn from politics as it is usually practiced on campus?

The experiment raises other questions for higher education because of its implications for research and teaching. Harriger and McMillan explain that despite considerable experience, the experiment took them outside their comfort level. Teaching styles were the first thing to be challenged when they moderated deliberative forums. The interactions among students are all important in deliberation, and the professors had to find ways to foster deliberation without guiding the conversation. The two scholars also encountered tensions between their traditional role as researchers producing objective, expert knowledge and their undefined role when students and citizens working to create the kind of knowledge needed to inform their decisions. Harriger's and McMillan's knowledge of their disciplines wasn't irrelevant, but its relation to the knowledge in deliberation wasn't clear. They had entered the yet-to-be-charted realm of public scholarship and had to deal with the tension between being detached scholars and caring citizens. Their report on how they met these challenges is refreshingly personal, candid, and devoid of easy answers. And their account of what they discovered about themselves and the canons of academe will be invaluable to other teachers and scholars who undertake similar experiments.

While the significance of the Wake Forest experiment is clear, there hasn't been enough time to judge its impact. As this book goes to press, no one knows how Wake Forest University will respond. But this decision isn't for one institution alone. The way colleges and universities relate to the democratic enterprise and the challenges of self-government has always gone a long way toward establishing their identity. That was true of the colonial colleges, whose students made them "seminaries of sedition"; it was true of the land-grant institutions that defined themselves as the "people's colleges"; and it has been true of what were once called junior colleges, which have found their true identity in "community." As I said earlier, the question is how these institutions define themselves today. A higher education is now the key to personal success in the marketplace, and the pressure of preparing young people to succeed in their chosen professions is considerable. This preparation also has to be available at a competitive price, which puts an even greater premium on efficient management of scarce resources. In meeting all these demands, I hope higher education won't forget that it was once itself a civic movement. The most significant contribution of the Wake Forest experiment has been to refresh that memory—and keep it in the catalog.

—**David Mathews, President**
Kettering Foundation

CHAPTER ONE

Why College Students?
Why Deliberation?

Chapter One

Why College Students?
Why Deliberation?

I n the fall semester of 2001, we began a journey that would
take us through four years of experimentation with deliberative
democracy in a campus setting with 30 entering first-year students
at our liberal arts university. We called the group "Democracy
Fellows," and we worked with them in the classroom, on campus,
and in the wider community as we explored together the joys,
challenges, and just plain hard work that come with democratic
processes. Only a few weeks into that first year, as we gathered
for our morning seminar, two planes crashed into the World Trade
Center towers in New York City and, no doubt, changed forever
the context within which we would study young people and their
civic engagement. While we were at a loss to explain what was
happening on that fateful day, it did occur to us—and we shared the
thought with our students—that the violence we were witnessing
was almost invariably preceded by a breakdown in civil political
discourse, the very enterprise these students were studying. A "war
on terrorism" followed, as did the war in Iraq. During their senior
year in 2004, as students ended their tenure as Democracy Fellows,
a divisive presidential election occurred. The world does not stand
still while researchers conduct their controlled studies. Such is the
nature of social-science research.

This is the story of the four years we spent with the Democracy
Fellows. In it we speak in several voices. We are the social-science
researchers, attempting to measure the impact of deliberative
interventions with a group of college students and to frame that
research in the larger context of our disciplines of political science
and communication. We are the teachers who sought to teach the
students not only the theory and concepts of democracy, but also
the democratic skills and sensibilities that would serve them as
citizens in a democratic society. And finally, we are ourselves
citizens of our university and larger communities who feel an

obligation to engage with those communities through processes that are both democratic and respectful.

There are other voices speaking in this story as well. They are the Democracy Fellows, as well as other students who were not in the program. Throughout the four years, we captured their voices through individual interviews, focus groups, and writing assignments. To the extent possible, we have used these voices to help us tell this story. In the end, this is the story of how a group of students learned what we call in this work a set of "democratic sensibilities"—what one advocate of deliberative democracy calls "the discipline to keep an open mind, the willingness to stand in someone else's shoes, the capacity to change, and the ability to make decisions with others" (Mathews 1997, 16).

Defining the Problem

For several decades, scholars and practitioners have been concerned about the decline of political, and more broadly, civic engagement among U.S. citizens. Declining voter turnout, polls showing alienation from public life and cynicism about politics and politicians, and evidence of significant lack of knowledge of, and interest in, politics have all raised concerns in both the political science and communication disciplines about the health of American democracy (Arnett and Arneson 1999; Asen 2004; Hauser 1999; Ivie 1998; Mann and Patrick 2000; Putnam 2000; Sproule 2002). This disengagement appears to be especially high among young people. While voter turnout is low across all age groups, it is lowest for the youngest voting cohort. Even more important are the attitudes that lead to low levels of participation. In her analysis of young Americans, Carol Hays (1998, 45) concludes that *alienation*—a catchall term combining cynicism, distrust, lack of efficacy, and apathy—is "the most widespread characterization of this generation." While adults tend to feel anger toward politics, work in the 1990s showed that younger voters felt pessimistic and disconnected (The Harwood Group 1993; Johnson, Hays, and Hays 1998, 219). The 2000 Higher Education Research Institute

(HERI) annual survey of college freshmen provided further confirmation of this trend, reporting that student interest in politics was at an all-time low for an election year (Sax, Astin, Korn, and Mahoney 2001). More recent data indicate a slight up-swing, suggesting that perhaps this trend has bottomed out and a new generation of "millennial" students (Lowry and Strauss 2001) may be developing more interest in politics in the aftermath of September 11, 2001. Certainly, the presidential election of 2004 provided some evidence that more young people could be mobilized to participate in a critical election (HERI 2004b; Patterson 2004). However, even with this upward turn, interest in politics and political engagement is still half of what it was for young people when freshmen surveys began in the 1960s (Rooney 2003). Furthermore, the 2004 HERI survey showed that students who *are* engaged are mirroring the polarization found in the larger electorate (HERI 2004a), pointing to another set of issues about what *kind* of engagement democratic citizens employ. Robert Putnam (2000) also finds declining involvement in this youth cohort across a number of measures of civic engagement.

Civic Renewal, Higher Education, and Deliberation

In response to these troubling trends, those working in the area of civic renewal have pursued multiple ways of thinking about the problem and approaches to reengaging young people in political life. Two particular concerns in this movement inform this research. The first is the role that higher education can and should play in encouraging engaged citizenship. (See, for example, Colby, Ehrlich, Beaumont, and Stephens 2003; Englund 2002; Galston 2003; Gutmann 1987; Kettering Foundation 1992; London 2000; McDonnell, Timpane, and Benjamin 2000; Nie, Junn, and Stehlik-Barry 1996; Nussbaum 1997; Walker 2002.) Regardless of the course of action they advocate, many scholars agree with Woodruff Smith that, "for better or worse, American public higher education, the American public sphere, and American democracy rise and fall together" (2003, 69).

The second concern motivating this work is an interest in the value of deliberation and the positive effects opportunities to deliberate about public issues can have on political attitudes and behavior (Button and Ryfe 2005; Delli Carpini, Cook, and Jacob 2004). Though the notion of deliberation is a contested one, when we speak of deliberation, we mean a particular kind of conversation in which participants weigh the costs and consequences of various choices against what they consider most valuable. (See Burkhalter, Gastil, and Kelshaw 2002, for a recent effort toward definitional and theoretical clarity.) Public deliberation allows people to discover what concerns them most, what they are and are not willing to do about a problem, and what trade-offs they are willing to accept. The goal is progress toward a shared sense of direction or purpose, not consensus or complete agreement on any solution. The deliberative model features talk that involves listening as well as speaking, considering the experiences and underlying values of others, and structuring the conversation in such a way as to afford equal status for all participants (Delli Carpini, Cook, and Jacobs 2004).

Most scholars who support public deliberation argue that it is essential to a more legitimate participatory democracy, and that, as McLeod, et al. (1999, 744) conclude: "It is only through this constant give-and-take relationship that citizens can develop a fuller understanding of their own position and the various positions held by others within the community." Gastil and Dillard (1999b) conclude that deliberative discussions foster a general sophistication in political judgment. Other scholars argue that deliberation improves the political climate by informing the population about current issues, promoting reasoning skills, and ultimately forcing citizens to defend their views in the face of opposition (Stokes 1998). Deliberation also emphasizes thinking in terms of the common good rather than solely in terms of the individual, and thus results in policy outcomes that benefit a wider range of the population (Gambetta 1998). John Rawls argues that deliberation is bound up with citizenship:

> The ideal of citizenship imposes a moral, not a legal, duty
> —the duty of civility—to be able to explain to one another

on those fundamental questions how the principles and policies they advocate and vote for can be supported by the political values of public reason. This duty also involves a willingness to listen to others and a fairmindedness in deciding when accommodations to their views should reasonably be made (1993, 217).

Theorists of participatory democracy emphasize the educative function of participation and, for many of them, deliberation is one of the most important means by which this learning occurs. This view assumes that the very act of participation *teaches*, as citizens learn what it means to be part of a public (Barber 1984; Pateman 1970). While Gastil and Dillard stop short of claiming a direct correlation between deliberating in National Issues Forums (NIF)[8] forums and political participation, they did find that NIF can bolster participants' political efficacy, refine their political judgments, broaden their political conversation networks, and reduce their conversational dominance (1999a, 179). Barbaras (2004, 699) found that deliberation can have the positive effect of encouraging citizens to "discard their inaccurate factual perceptions as well as rigidly held political views." Finally, Benjamin Barber argues that a strong (participatory) democracy that includes deliberative opportunities can "overcome the pessimism and cynicism" that many citizens feel (1984, 119).

Deliberation is not without its critics. The practice has the potential to force homogeneity on heterogeneous communities and can slow community response and adaptation to change. There is always the possibility that stronger, more eloquent, better informed community members will unfairly influence weaker participants and the increased likelihood that some discussants will perpetuate inaccurate information (Deetz 1999; Gambetta 1998; Janis 1989). When people are misled by a particularly eloquent speaker, Przeworski terms it *indoctrination* and argues that it can

---

[8] NIF is a nationwide network of civic and educational organizations whose common interest is to promote nonpartisan deliberation on public issues. See Melville, Willingham, and Dedrick (2005) for a comprehensive description of the function and impact of the NIF network.

lead people "to hold beliefs that are not in their best interest" (1998, 140-141). There is a possibility that citizens will resist the opportunity to deliberate (Hibbing and Theiss-Morse 2002) or that deliberation on extremely contentious issues will simply lead to no solution at all (Shapiro 1999, 28-38).

"Difference democrats" (see, for example, Mouffe 1999; Young 1997) have waged a particularly compelling attack on deliberation. Some scholars (Bell 1999, 70-87; Bohman 1996, 16; McLeod, et al. 1999; Sanders 1997; Schauer 1999, 22) argue that the pluralism of contemporary society precludes the possibility of equal representation and participation that is required by the "ideal speech situation" (Habermas 1984). More consonant with our national diversity, argues Mouffe (1999), is "agonistic pluralism" which recognizes our forms of exclusion instead of rationalizing or moralizing them and keeps alive the "democratic contestation." (See also Ivie 1998.) Young (1997) adds that the narrowness of acceptable communicative forms in deliberation inherently excludes those not well versed in those skills. The "force of the better argument" (Habermas 1984) should be supplemented, in Young's view, by communicative forms to which there is wider access, such as greeting, rhetoric (which she defines as emotion and figurative speech), and storytelling. (See also, Ryfe 2006.) When discussion becomes only a "gentleman's club" (Dryzek 2000, 57), dominated by a well-informed, articulate faction, the result may be that weaker members feel less capable (Stokes 1998, 124). Deliberation among diverse groups can also deteriorate into ordinary, polarizing debate, which reinforces the alienating effects of politics (Shapiro 1999). But a lack of diversity in the group can also have a negative impact on deliberation, minimizing the ability of participants to learn and to change as a result of their experience (Ryfe 2005).

In our research we have attempted to take into account both the benefits and the potential limitations of deliberation. Review of the research literature reminds us that "Habermas may be correct that deliberation is a natural human talent, but it is not easy to cultivate and maintain" (Ryfe 2005, 60). We ask whether the positive transformative effects of learning to deliberate can be achieved through the teaching and training of young people in higher education. But we also ask how we can be aware of the potential problems of deliberation and how they might be ameliorated in that process. We acknowledge that much of the discussion of the proposed benefits and dangers of deliberation is untested and speculative. Our goal in this project is to contribute to the relatively new but growing efforts to test these various propositions through empirical research (Delli Carpini, Cook, and Jacob 2004; Ryfe 2005).

The concept of deliberation, as a method of increasing student civic engagement has gained standing. With regard to higher education, deliberation has been considered as a classroom tool (Campbell 2005; Doble, Peng, Frank, and Salim 1999; Ervin 1997), a method of campuswide communication (Mallory and Thomas 2003; Schoem and Hurtado 2002), and a means of promoting interaction with communities (Brisbin and Hunter 2003; Murphy 2004). In *Democratic Education*, Amy Gutmann (1987, 173) argues that "learning how to think carefully about political problems, to articulate one's views and defend them is a form of education for which universities are well suited."

As a classroom tool, deliberation provides a means of exposing students to important civic knowledge, skills, and experiences needed for citizenship. It teaches them "to critically examine evidence, to be able to see the world through multiple viewpoints— to step into other shoes; to make connections and see patterns" (Howell 2002, 117). Attempts to promote deliberative methods campuswide should be developed to include more than "sporadic public panel discussion and lectures, departmental meetings, or professional seminars," which typically represent the dialogue that occurs on college campuses (Mallory and Thomas 2003, 11), and should instead seek ways to involve students in wider governance processes when possible (Carey 2000; McMillan 2004; Morse 1993). Deliberative dialogue is a beneficial tool for linking students with communities outside of college campuses as well. Practicing public deliberation in communities could produce deliberative habits, develop necessary skills, and build political knowledge

(Burkhalter, Gastil, and Kelshaw 2002; Gastil and Dillard 1999a). Efforts to improve campus-community partnerships involve "more informed conversation between college and universities and collective organizations in the state or region surrounding the campus" (Brisbin and Hunter 2003, 485; Thomas 2000).

John J. Patrick (2000) identifies the key components of effective civic education that colleges and universities should consider in developing programs of this sort. These include the acquisition of *knowledge* of concepts, principles, and history of democracy and the role of citizens; the development of *cognitive skills* of identifying, describing, analyzing, explaining, evaluating, and thinking critically and constructively about what this substantive knowledge means for the way democracy works and our role in it; the development of *participatory skills,* such as interacting with others, monitoring public events, deliberating about public policy and influencing policy decisions; and finally, the encouragement of *dispositions of citizenship,* which include the promotion of the general welfare, recognition of the common humanity of each person, respecting and protecting rights, taking responsibility for one's participation, and supporting democratic principles and practices.

In this book, we consider the ways teaching college students the process of deliberation might contribute to their interest in, and the quality of, their participation in civic life. We have framed our study using the educational components identified by Patrick and the notion of *context*—the settings where deliberation might be used and the strengths and limitations of each venue for teaching students the democratic skill of deliberative talk. (See Huckfeldt 1979; Huckfeldt, Beck, Dalton, and Levine 1995; McLeod, et al. 1999 for discussions of the importance of context in assessing deliberation.)

The Research Design

In 2001, we began a longitudinal research project, which examined the experiences of a group of students as they made their way through four years of education at our private, liberal arts college in North Carolina. We were interested in exploring several interrelated questions that probe the role of higher education in civic education. We sought to understand:

- how the college experience itself shapes students' attitudes and behavior with regard to civic engagement. What is happening during this time that either encourages or discourages them to become involved in politics and in their communities?
- whether students who learned how to deliberate about public issues developed different sensibilities about their roles as democratic citizens than their peers who had not had this experience.
- the effects of context on the deliberative experience. Did it make a difference whether students deliberated with each other in the classroom, with their peers on campus, or with diverse citizens in the community?

We pursued these questions by gathering data from several sets of students. The first was a group of 30 students who were recruited from the entering class in the fall of 2001 to participate in the Democracy Fellows program. These students were enrolled in a first-year seminar entitled "Deliberative Democracy" and participated in various activities that provided them the opportunity to experiment with democratic decision making during their four-year careers. Later in this chapter, we will describe these fellows and their selection in more detail. During the first semester, we conducted entry interviews with all the fellows to establish a baseline of their political views. In subsequent years, they were interviewed in focus groups about their ongoing experiences with deliberation and campus life and were given a brief participation survey to gauge their political activities. In the senior year, we conducted exit interviews with them. All of these sessions were audiotaped and transcribed.

The second group of 30 students was randomly selected from a list of the entering class that *excluded* the 30 Democracy Fellows. We called this comparison group the "class cohort" (of the 30 invited, only 25 participated initially), and they were invited to participate in focus groups each year. While the original cohort served as the core group throughout the study, their numbers were supplemented, when necessary, to maintain a critical mass of non-fellow respondents from the class of 2001. In the first year, these students were asked the same questions that had been asked of the Democracy Fellows in the individual interviews. In subsequent years, we asked both the Democracy Fellows and the class cohort some of the same questions. In addition, we queried the Democracy Fellows about their experiences with deliberative activities, something the class cohort had not experienced. These interviews were audiotaped and transcribed.

During the second year of the study, we talked with a third group of students as well. These students were neither in the Democracy Fellows program nor part of the class cohort. They were students from all classes who participated in a campus deliberation planned and hosted by the Democracy Fellows in October of 2002. Again 30 students were invited and 25 attended focus groups where we asked them the same questions we asked the Democracy Fellows about their deliberative experience and administered the same participation survey that the fellows and cohort took.

When designing a research project, social scientists are always faced with challenging choices about what kind of data to gather and what methods to use in gathering and analyzing them. No approach is perfect and each choice both illuminates and obscures. Our decision to work with a small group of students on a single campus allowed us to go into considerable depth through interviews and focus groups and gave us a substantial amount of data in the authentic voices of the students. We recognize, of course, that in order to get that depth and specificity, we sacrificed breadth and sample size, which might have allowed us to make broader generalizations about college students. As a partial correction of this deficiency we used survey data that we gathered by adding questions to the Wake Forest campus surveys given to all entering freshmen and a sample of exiting seniors who served as subjects of the national HERI study of college students' attitudes. These data provide some insight into how our two sample groups compare to their Wake Forest peers.

The Setting

Wake Forest University is a private liberal arts college located in Winston-Salem, North Carolina. It was founded by the Baptist State Convention in 1854 and it maintained that relationship until 1986, when the Board of Trustees voted to become autonomous. In addition to the College of Arts and Sciences, the university includes an undergraduate business college, a law school, a graduate school of business, a divinity school, a graduate school of arts and sciences, and a medical school located on another campus in the city. In the spring of 2002, when the Democracy Fellows entered, there were 4,045 undergraduates on campus and the majority of first-year students were in the top 10 percent of their graduating classes in high school. The student body was predominantly white, with a minority student population of 12.2 percent. Although the campus is experiencing increasing diversity, the critical mass of the student population is affluent and leans toward political conservatism.

In contrast to its sleepy, small-town beginnings in eastern North Carolina, Wake Forest today is well known as one of the "small Ivies," consistently making a strong showing in the annual *US News and World Report* college rankings. Guided by its motto *"Pro Humanitate,"* the school has a storied history of weighing in on social and political battles, such as the evolution controversy, and has turned back several challenges to its strong stance on academic freedom. Wake Forest took a giant, but controversial, step in the leadership of higher education in 1995 when it struck a deal with technology giant, IBM, to become one of the first completely wired campuses in the country.

Wake Forest has not been exempt from the national concern over student public-mindedness, which we chronicled above. There have been varied efforts to respond to that concern, including the university's participation in the Kettering Foundation's Public Leadership Education Project, the strengthening and expansion of the Volunteer Service Corps (VSC), collaboration between the VSC and the Teaching and Learning Center to promote service learning across the curriculum, and recently, some preliminary efforts to encourage more public deliberation in addressing campus-life issues. Therefore for the purposes of this study, it is important to note that given its culture and history and anchored by its motto *"Pro Humanitate,"* Wake Forest *should* be a campus amenable to the process of deliberation. Other campuses would undoubtedly face different, perhaps more formidable, challenges. It is our hope that schools of different sizes, populations, and even educational philosophies will benefit from our experiment and, in particular, will test and refine our methods to ensure a more successful deliberative future for higher education.

Who Were the Democracy Fellows?

Without betraying the confidentiality that the students were promised and the Institutional Review Board requires, we would like the reader to know as much as possible about the Democracy Fellows. First, the Admissions Office provided us with a demographic breakdown of the entering class of 2001 so that, in selecting the fellows, we could seek a relatively representative sample of entering students, at least in some categories. Over the summer of 2001, we contacted each first-year student with information about the Democracy Fellows program and suggested the possibility that he or she might opt to apply for the program and thereby choose Deliberative Democracy as the first-year seminar. In addition to asking for demographic information used to align the applicants with the larger class profile, we asked applicants to list their most significant high-school activities, to reflect on the requirements of citizenship, to describe their memorable experiences in working with a group, and to tell us what they expected to contribute to the Democracy Fellows group they were proposing to join.

We received 60 applications for the 30 available slots, a number fixed by the fact that we could only offer two sections of the first-year seminar and these courses were limited to 15 students per section. After each researcher carefully read each application, we sorted them according to the parameters of the class with regard to gender, minority status, and geographical diversity. Then we considered the additional information the applicants had given us. The selection of the final 30 was ultimately determined by insightfulness of the application, varied high-school activities, unique perspectives, openness to learning a new perspective, and a balanced mixture of liberal and conservative viewpoints. Despite the fact that in the overall group there appeared to be a bias that politics matters, several of the students admitted to not having acted on that presumption. In fact, we intentionally took some students whose high-school activities and self-professed assessment reflected little or no political zeal and, in a number of cases, we eliminated from the pool some students who had been extremely active politically.

In the group of 30 Democracy Fellows chosen, there were 15 males and 15 females, with 8 minority students. Slightly more than half (18) were from the Southeast, with 6 of them from North Carolina. There were six students from the Mid-Atlantic states, three from the Midwest, two from New England, and one from Texas. Thus, in terms of demographics, the group mirrored fairly well the overall make-up of the entering class.

While all of the applicants professed some level of interest in politics and citizen engagement, there was variation in the degree to which their "most significant" high-school activities reflected that interest. Still many of the students' reports contained activities that were tacit, if not explicit, examples of citizenship:

- 11 students listed student-government activities; about half had held an office
- 13 listed community-service projects of one sort or another
- 6 listed active participation on debate teams
- 6 others listed an assortment of activities that have political content of some sort: model UN, political science club, youth membership on the city council, a city-sponsored multicultural leadership program, and a national office in the Future Business Leaders of America

Philosophically, the students who were selected seemed relatively similar in answering what they thought citizenship requires:

paying attention to public affairs and voting, themes which might be encapsulated in a sense of responsibility, which many referenced. Beyond those commonalities, however, were some interesting variations, which we sought to capture in the selection process—for example, the differences between "passive" and "active" citizenship; individualism versus community; and the role and functions of voice. Most students clearly felt that they would contribute to the group with life experiences, leadership skills, and public speaking and debating experiences (several told us that they liked to "argue" about politics). Not surprisingly few, if any, seemed to think of public talk in deliberative ways.

Summary of Findings

What we found, in brief, was that when they left Wake Forest after four years, the Democracy Fellows were more interested and engaged politically than a comparison group in these specific ways: they were more involved in traditional political venues, more expressive of the responsibilities of citizenship, more analytical and critical of political processes, more efficacious in their political attitudes and language, more communal in political language and outlook, and more imaginative in recognizing possibilities for deliberation and its broader application. Furthermore, we learned that even limited exposure to deliberation, less frequent and less formal, also delivers at least trace amounts of those same benefits that were prominent among the Democracy Fellows.

The exit data gathered annually from the senior class by the Higher Education Research Institute and the WFU Office of Institutional Research offers another interesting finding: because this survey allowed us to contrast the Democracy Fellows, the class cohort, and the senior class as a whole, we were able to discern the relative impact of deliberative exposure. As we will describe more specifically in Chapter Six, the Democracy Fellows separated themselves from both the cohort and the class-at-large on two important measures: their perceptions of voice and their belief that their college education, which had featured intensive deliberative training, had prepared them for active citizenship. However, the students in the cohort with their limited focus group exposure, were more positive on these measures than the class-at-large, reinforcing the qualitative data on the benefits of *any* deliberative experience. Finally, we found that the contexts available to colleges—the classroom, the campus, and the larger community—do make a difference in students' learning and that each offers both benefits and limitations in teaching students to become active citizens.

The Plan of the Book

We will explicate the findings previewed above first by examining the entering expectations of the Democracy Fellows and their first-year class cohort. What experiences that shaped their views about politics and their expectations about the college experience did they bring to campus? We explore the phenomenon we call "citizenship deferred"—a notion we found within both groups that politics and citizenship are not something they can and should do now, but instead something they'll get to, maybe, sometime later in their lives. (See also, Campus Compact 2002; Loeb 1994.)

The next three chapters explore the impact of the three delibera-tive interventions that the Democracy Fellows experienced during their first three years: a first-year seminar, in which they learned and practiced deliberative skills; a campus deliberation, which they planned and executed during their sophomore year; and a community deliberation, which they organized in Winston-Salem during their junior year. In each we consider what we learned about that particular context for deliberation in terms of its benefits and/or drawbacks for developing democratic sensibilities in the students. In Chapter Six, we discuss the senior-year data, comparing the Democracy Fellows to their senior cohort. After four years, which experiences seem most powerful? Which aspects of the college experience have been most significant for both groups? As they enter the working world, will they continue to defer their citizenship or will they embrace it?

We speak to the wider applicability of our study in two chapters of the book. We summarize our major findings and explore how they either confirm or modify received traditions about the political development of college students—or offer some totally new insights. Finally, given what we learned, what can and should colleges and universities do to develop democratic citizens? What can higher education bring to the civic-renewal movement?

CHAPTER TWO

Citizenship Deferred

Chapter Two

Citizenship Deferred

As colleges and universities consider whether and how to prepare their students for citizenship, it seems worthwhile to know what they are working with and where students are when they begin their college experience. So we began our research by inquiring about our students' attitudes toward politics and civic engagement. What experiences had they already had that affected their interest in, or distaste for, politics? How were they expecting their college experience to influence their citizenship, both while they were in college and after they graduated? How did they think colleges and universities might best prepare students to be engaged citizens?

To make this preliminary assessment, we gathered data from three sources: We conducted individual interviews with the Democracy Fellows; we asked the same questions of a comparison group of entering students gathered in focus groups; and we added three questions about civic engagement and college expectations to the annual local survey given to first-year students as part of HERI's annual collection of data on college students. We repeated these same questions in our individual interviews and focus groups so that we could compare both groups to the whole class.

Many scholars of civic engagement have been interested in the question of how young people come to develop political sensibilities and the impact of that early socialization on their adult political behavior. Before looking at the data we gathered, it is worth noting what they have to say. Socialization scholars tend to agree on a few key premises. First, they find that civic training in adolescence has a significant impact on adult civic behavior and the development of civic and democratic competencies (McLellan and Youniss 1997; Verba, Schlozman, and Brady 1995). Second, they know that the process of socialization is a complex interaction of schooling, family, and community influences (Andolina, Jenkins, Zukin, and Keeter 2003).

On the other hand, because the issue of youth socialization has been studied in a number of different disciplines (human development, community development, political science, psychology, education) without much conversation among these scholars, there has been little effort, until recently, to identify where the findings of these diverse scholars overlap and to provide a fuller picture of the process (Gibson 2001). It seems clear that school-based civic education alone cannot do the work of adequately socializing young people. While teachers who encourage open discussion of political issues in the classroom can have a significant impact on civic learning (Gimpel, Lay, and Schuknecht 2003), active family involvement in politics and community-based programs and opportunities for active learning are critically important as well (Andolina, Jenkins, Zukin, and Keeter 2003; Sherrod, Flanagan, and Youniss 2002). A survey of the key literature in this area concluded that "students need face-to-face interpersonal experiences, need to take part in groups that advance the public good and incorporate them into social networks, and need to acquire knowledge that will prepare them for participation in the political system" (Gibson 2001, 15).

These findings suggest several things relevant to our assessment of entering college students. Researchers should expect to find variation among the students in terms of their knowledge, interest, and commitment to political engagement, which is tied to their adolescent experiences at home, in school, and in their communities. Students likely will arrive on campus with already deeply planted seeds of engagement, disinterest, alienation, or hostility to politics and civic life. Further, their expectations about college life with regard to civic education most likely will be shaped by what they have already experienced. Clearly, colleges and universities would do well to heed this youth socialization literature in constructing any program of civic engagement, recognizing the complex intersection of knowledge acquisition and experiential learning that appears to be the key to encouraging involvement by young people.

Attitudes about Politics and Civic Engagement

We found little difference between the Democracy Fellows and the comparison group when it came to their general assessments of the state of politics in the United States today. While both groups were optimistic about the basic soundness of the system, they tended to feel little sense of efficacy, defined by scholars of participation as "a sense of personal competence in one's ability to understand politics and to participate in politics . . . as well as a sense that one's political activities can influence what the government actually does" (Rosenstone and Hansen 1993, 15). They also shared a concern about intense partisanship and the role of money in politics.

Optimism and patriotism. The students in both samples assessed the American political system as basically sound and requiring little change. They tended to believe that it worked relatively well, especially in comparison to many other countries' systems. For example, 93 percent of Democracy Fellows had confidence that the political system worked very well (30 percent) or somewhat well (63 percent). In the comparison group, 48 percent had a "great deal" of confidence that the political system works and another 44 percent were "somewhat" confident in its soundness. A number of the students praised and defended the system as the best there is. (All of the focus groups met post-September 11, and, as a consequence, there may well have been much more patriotism expressed than might have been felt at another time.) The overriding theme seemed to be a kind of complacency about the system and an assumption that things were as they should be. One student in the comparison group said:

> I don't think it could be that bad. Maybe a lot of people aren't involved or anything, but at the same time people aren't involved on a lot of levels. I guess because we're happy, we're content here. I guess the main goal of politics is running our country and if the general public is content . . . I don't know if that is an ignorant thing to say, but we're pretty much content so it can't be doing too much too wrong.

Another student argued that the system was:

working exactly how it should . . . like the founders wanted
it to. It is perpetuating the status quo unless the status quo
is wrong and then you can change it, but I see it as just like
this is how it is supposed to be. It might be a little bad [to
say] but for the most part . . . there are very few issues that
are very wrong.

Dislike for partisan politics. Students were most dissatisfied
with the role played by political parties in the political system.
They expressed the belief that parties force people to vote against
their individual beliefs, and they wished for a system in which
everyone voted their conscience and no one was controlled by
party leadership. Across the board they expressed a distaste
for partisan conflict and the negativity it brings to politics. The
comments of one Democracy Fellow summarized this theme:

I wish that our system wasn't so partisan; I kind of wish
there were a lot of independents, or at least a third party.
A true third party, because I hate things being so black and
white, Republican, Democrat, Conservative, and Liberal.
An independent individualistic person would be a good
role model and a good person in politics, but you can't
even have individualism in politics because they are so
engulfed in the partisanship.

Money and politics. Students were also worried about the
role of money in politics, although this was mentioned less often
than political parties. They thought that money advantages special
interests over average citizens and that one cannot have an impact
in politics without money. For example, one student in the comparison group believed that "if you want to be elected you are going
to have to have lots of money and support of certain individuals.
You may have to promise them things and I don't think that is
how politics is supposed to work. . . . You do things for the people
in general, not just certain people." For many, this belief that
money controls politics made them less inclined to be involved.

Lack of efficacy. Most of the students in both groups expressed
very little sense of efficacy in affecting the political system, although

this sentiment was stronger in the comparison group than among the Democracy Fellows. The students attributed the absence of efficacy to a combination of their youth, the lack of relevance of issues to their lives, their lack of knowledge of how the system works, and the influence of more powerful, moneyed actors. One Democracy Fellow captured all of these sentiments when he said:

> I just think that as of right now there is not much that I can offer. . . . What I need to be doing is learning and figuring out what my role is and just figuring out what my views are because I'm not really sure of a lot of things. Besides voting, I think that is pretty much the only thing I can do now. . . . It is kind of hard if you don't have money and you don't have the power and the prestige to really get involved and to make a difference.

Another Democracy Fellow tied her general sense of inefficacy to the events of September 11, 2001, saying:

> If I was asked three days ago, I might have been more optimistic about what was happening, but I just don't think that the individual matters as much as they used to. And I think America is just getting too large for people to really have a clear voice and be able to do anything. . . . Really, no one is in charge and what is going to happen is going to happen. . . . It is just another way that it sort of makes me feel out of the loop.

Comparison-group students were even more likely to talk about civic engagement as something beyond their capacity. When we asked both groups to identify their own level of involvement and interest in being active citizens, 33 percent of Democracy Fellows considered themselves to be very active participants in politics while only 12 percent of the comparison group did. At the bottom of the scale, 36 percent of comparison-group participants identified themselves as barely, or not at all, active while only 20 percent of Democracy Fellows classified themselves in this way.

There were students in both groups who saw things differently. One young woman in the Democracy Fellows program whose parents are immigrants was much more certain about the importance of being an engaged college student. Referring to a quotation she had seen in *Time* magazine about politics being "a bow of idealism," she said, "That is probably what fascinates me about politics . . . that everyday citizens can shoot their political ideas and they can actually see them go into action. Just the fact that even though I am only 18 years old, I can even be politically involved." But even this young woman expressed some alienation from government: "People feel estranged from the federal government," she said, ". . . because they are in Washington, D.C., and we're all so far removed from them, and then they do their own thing in the White House and on Capitol Hill and very seldom do we actually realize what is going on up there."

Influential High-School Experiences

The literature on political socialization shows that, although it is not the exclusive factor affecting young people's political engagement, their educational experiences are important in shaping their involvement. We found this to be true in both groups of students we interviewed. Furthermore, educational experiences could have both a positive or negative impact on their interest and engagement with politics.

Students who had had experiences with active learning in a simulated or actual political setting were the most likely to feel positive about civic engagement and to express the desire to become active citizens. Experiences like debate, model legislatures, model UN, service on government decision-making bodies, or employment as a page in a legislative body all contributed positively to students' attitudes about engagement.

Students who were excited about politics and civic engagement were more likely to have had teachers and civics classes that used active and experiential learning as part of the class. Conversely, some very negative attitudes about politics and engagement were, at least in part, the result of boring social-studies classes involving rote memorization of textbook material.

Student government associations in the high-school setting
rarely taught positive lessons about politics and engagement to
these students. With very few exceptions, students dismissed
them as "popularity contests" with "no influence" that had, in
many cases, made them cynical about elected leadership and
student power.

Expectations for College

The central theme of all WFU students' expectations about
their college experience was that they expected studying, campus
activities, and being with friends to leave them very little time for
engagement with campus and community issues. They spoke of
citizenship as something to be deferred until after they left college.
The one place they did imagine exposure to political ideas and
concepts was in the traditional classroom setting. Students were
least likely to think they would have a voice in campus governance,
attributing this to various causes, including lack of time, lack of
interest, and lack of confidence in student influence.

Table 1 demonstrates that Democracy Fellows entered college
with generally higher expectations of involvement than their
peers across three dimensions we asked about: community service,
campus governance, and their education for active citizenship.
The comparison and Democracy Fellows groups were more alike
than the overall class with the biggest difference being the expectation of having a voice in campus governance. We believe that
the difference shown by the Democracy Fellows on campus governance and civic education dimensions can be explained largely by
their expectation of what they would gain from the Democracy
Fellows program. It is notable that all three groups expected fairly
high levels of involvement with community service, mirroring
trends that have been identified in a number of studies suggesting
that community service is the "new politics" of this generation
(Campus Compact 2002; National Association of Secretaries of
State 1998; Putnam 2000; Rimmerman 2005).

Table 1
Expectations of Campus Experience

Community Service[a]			
	All WFU (N 870)	Class Cohort (N 25)	Democracy Fellows (N 30)
Great Deal	27.2%	40%	50%
Somewhat	46.1%	60%	40%
Unsure	20.4%	0%	10%
Not at All	4.8%	0%	0%

Campus Governance[b]			
	All WFU (N 870)	Class Cohort (N 25)	Democracy Fellows (N 30)
Great Deal	7%	0%	20%
Somewhat	25.9%	64%	50%
Unsure	33.8%	32%	27%
Not at All	24.8%	4%	3%

Civic Preparedness[c]			
	All WFU (N 870)	Class Cohort (N 25)	Democracy Fellows (N 30)
Great Deal	34.5%	52%	60%
Somewhat	37.2%	44%	30%
Unsure	20.1%	4%	10%
Not at All	6.4%	0%	0%

[a] To what degree do you expect to be involved in community service during your time at Wake Forest?

[b] To what degree do you expect to have a voice in campus governance while at Wake Forest?

[c] To what degree do you expect your education to prepare you to be a politically active citizen?

Note: The "All WFU" category includes responses from students in the other two groups. The class cohort and the Democracy Fellows were administered separate surveys in order to single out their responses.

Citizenship deferred. While the survey results from the entire first-year class and our two study groups demonstrated that, particularly among Democracy Fellows, there were many students who expected to be involved citizens of the campus community, when we probed further, Democracy Fellows expressed more ambivalence about whether they would actually be engaged in activities that prepare them for active citizenship. Despite the fact that they were in a special program designed for this very purpose, many of them imagined college as a time when they were relatively inactive politically as the many other activities available to them vied for their attention. They also tended to think of politics and citizenship as subject-specific and therefore their involvement might be dependent on whether they chose to study these particular topics. One Democracy Fellow believed that his involvement would "depend on what I major in. If I take purely science classes, if I'm going to do chemistry, there is not really a lot of room for a political education. Right now, I think that if I'm going to be a science major then it is probably going to close some of the doors to being politically active." Another said that he did not know:

> . . . how involved I will be because there are going to be so many time constraints with homework and class and, you know, crew, and everything like that. I'd like to make an impact and help people in the community, but I don't know how much time I'll be able to devote to that while doing other things that I'll be able to do while I'm in college. You can always do community service but you can't always do . . . certain other things that can only happen in these four years.

The sense that politics is something for others to engage in while they focus on college life was even stronger among the class cohort. "I can't say I have an interest in everything that goes on," one first-year student said. "Especially when you are here at Wake Forest, you lose touch with what is happening. That is not to say that I don't care what happens, but I guess I trust those people that whatever happens will be for the good." Another comparison-group student identified politics and citizenship activities as something that some people "have an aptitude for" while others do not.

Learning about politics. On the other hand, many of the students did see college as a time when their opinions and attitudes about political matters would be further shaped and developed. Of the fellows, 60 percent believed that their education would prepare them "a great deal" to be active citizens and another 30 percent thought it would have "some" impact in that direction. This percentage is significantly higher than the whole class where 34.5 percent answered "a great deal" and 37.2 percent answered "somewhat." Fellows imagined that through the classroom, discussions with peers, and the deliberative democracy program of which they were a part, they would learn more about what they thought about issues. But this learning process was envisioned more as a traditional intake of information than as the result of learning through action. One Democracy Fellow noted that:

> Probably the main reason I came to college is [that] I think people should go to college to have their ideas and what they think about the world and life challenged. They should be forced to think about them and reorganize or completely get a new set of beliefs of what they think. I'm definitely hoping it happens here.

Another said:

> I think it is one of the roles of higher education and getting a good liberal arts education that lets you be exposed to a lot of areas of government and a lot of different subjects so that you can make a more informed decision. . . . Just being exposed to a lot of different types of information will help me get my personal views together.

Student Advice to Colleges and Universities

Because of our interest in what colleges and universities can do to encourage civic engagement, we asked students in both our study groups to consider four possible models for higher education's role in civic education (Kettering Foundation 1992). They are the *traditional academic model*, focusing on the classroom transfer of liberal arts knowledge, the *community service model*, focusing on volunteering in the community and service learning, the *teaching democratic skills model*, focusing on classroom or campus activities that teach students how to deliberate about issues together, and the *democratizing campus model*, which makes campus governance more democratic by giving students a real voice in the process. We asked the students what they thought about the strengths and weaknesses of each of the models as a way to encourage more civic engagement.

Traditional academic model. It was interesting to discover that despite their sense that the primary way they would learn citizenship at college would be through acquiring knowledge in the classroom, few of the students believed that the traditional academic model would be a successful way to impact college students' attitudes about political engagement. Their primary critique of the traditional academic model was that it is "more of the same" and therefore unlikely to increase involvement among those already disinclined to participate. One student in the comparison group said, "The people influenced by this model will be the same people who end up participating anyway. I definitely think it's a start and it can't hurt anything, but I don't see that as being a major solution to the problem of getting those who don't participate regularly to participate." Another from this class cohort argued that it would not "work as intended because that is the kind of education we received in high school, you go to class and you learn all these things, you leave high school, but are we more prepared to be an actively engaged citizen? No."

Interestingly, those who favored this model tended to do so for different reasons—either because it gave students the freedom to make their own decisions about engagement or because it coerced them into learning things they needed to learn to be good citizens. A comparison-group student endorsed the traditional classroom model because, "I'm not going to be affected much by proselytizing political views, and this model would be more you can let the individual decide for themselves once they become more educated." But another from the same group preferred this model because it seemed more motivational. She said:

> I think it is actually pretty good. . . . All students are slightly lazy and if they are forced to do it then it will happen. The classroom advantage is that there is a grade attached to it,

as terrible as that sounds. If you want to get the grade, which most kids do, you're going to have to participate and let your voice be heard in class, and by listening to other voices, listening and talking, then without a doubt you are going to want to become a better citizen.

Community service model. As we might expect, given national surveys that show an increased interest in community service among young people (National Association of Secretaries of State 1998; Sax, Astin, Korn, and Mahoney 2000) and their own expectations about being involved in community service as shown in Table 1, our students tended to like the community service model as a way to get people engaged in their communities. Reflecting the views expressed by many of them, a student from the comparison group said:

> This is a good model because if you actually go out and experience what is happening in the world and you actually go out of your little shelter, your bubble of Wake Forest, you can actually see what is going on in the world. I think that makes you care. Immediately you think if I'm making a difference on this kind of level just by going in and reading to a kid or helping a child learn how to read, then imagine what I can do on a larger scale.

The students in both study groups were much more skeptical about whether this model would produce *politically* engaged citizens and were particularly opposed to the notion of requiring such service, as they believed coercion would backfire. One Democracy Fellow noted, for example:

> Service is seen a lot of times as a one time thing that makes you feel good, and a lot of times people want to get involved with something that immediately they can see the results of their work as opposed to something that is helpful but you just can't really see it. . . . I think that community service is just something that people use to get the same feeling that they should be getting from being politically active and since they can't get that politically active, they resort to community service.

Another fellow said, "I don't agree with this one [the community service model]. I think it's kind of like two very different things that don't overlap to a great extent, except maybe some in local politics. People would just volunteer more time in soup kitchens rather than voting. I am against forcing them. It could turn them off more."

Teaching democratic skills. When we asked students about teaching democratic skills, such as deliberation, the Democracy Fellows immediately recognized this model as the one we were pursuing in our first-year seminar. We feared that they might be hesitant to critique the model given their involvement, and this may or may not have been the case. Some were willing to point to particular drawbacks, but most seemed to regard it as a good model because it combined the traditional acquisition of class- room knowledge with experiential learning of important skills. This preference for knowledge *and* practice was true of the class cohort as well, suggesting that it was not just familiarity with the model driving the Democracy Fellows' responses. Both groups identified similar strengths and drawbacks. In supporting the model, one student from the class cohort said:

> I think this is a good approach . . . especially looking at all of the other approaches. Talking about things makes you aware of other's opinions, other people's backgrounds and makes you more tolerant and aware of a lot of different issues. Also, it is a model that could be taught in high school and other settings.

Another favorable view from this group emphasized that deliber- ative skills are something that must be taught and therefore are appropriate to the educational setting:

> This [the democratic skills model] is good because I think being a citizen is . . . I don't think it is something you are. You almost have to learn it in a way. I think with having these skills the better citizen you become. Some people can deliberate but some can't. That is a skill they need to be taught and learn.

Despite the generally favorable view of this model, there were skeptics in both groups who identified limitations to this approach. One of the Democracy Fellows identified what some saw as the major drawback of the model: that it would have limited transferability outside of the classroom because of the time and effort required to deliberate. He said, "This won't have much effect outside the classroom because people have less and less time and I think they just have less and less enthusiasm to do those things once they get a job and once they are busy with family and work and everything. Voting is the main political outlet." Another fellow objected to the idea that citizenship could even be taught, saying "I just want to say I don't think you can teach someone to be a citizen. It is a decision you have to make. . . . I think there are people who are going to choose not to be a citizen and I don't see any way that college can train people to be citizens." This theme of individual choice was a popular one among the comparison-group students as well, as exemplified by one young man who said:

> You also have to be careful because if you let college or anyone try and teach you how to be a citizen, you're going to get this is how you should be and you're going to start confining people. You need the well-rounded population in a sense so if you start teaching just those certain things, if you start teaching to be a certain kind of citizen, you're going to be limiting.

Democratizing campus model. Finally, we asked the students to consider the possibility of democratizing the campus and giving students, as one group of stakeholders, more real say in decisions made by the university. Of the four models, this one probably received the greatest variation of responses, ranging from great enthusiasm to deep skepticism about whether students are sufficiently capable or willing to take on the responsibilities associated with this model. A supporter of the model from the class cohort said:

> This is probably the most important idea out of all of them . . . the fact that the college itself, if it expects to foster that kind of political education and expects to produce citizens that will actually go out and become politically involved, they have to have the model here. I think that college is like the bridge between high school where you are completely under the shelter of your parents and the bridge to the real world. I think it is such a crucial time to teach people that they can be politically involved.

A more cynical student in this group disliked the model because he thought that "students might get too rowdy. It could just turn into a popularity contest." Most common were student responses that were more ambivalent, seeing the appeal of the model but worrying about its potential dangers. One Democracy Fellow, for example said:

> I think in some way excluding students from decisions has an effect just by embittering them about the democratic process. They are just used to not voting and not being turned on to politics and I think on the majority it would have a negative effect at least if they are in a hierarchical institution. If, on the other hand, the university is very democratic . . . it could disillusion students when they got out in the real world to see [that] they don't have as much of an effect as they did in college.

And another student from the comparison group found it "an interesting idea and very intriguing." But, he said, "I don't know if it would work. In some instances, it would be a hassle I think because we have so much to do. Most of us have so much on our plates as it is and if you were to throw another heap of something on there . . . the upside would be that you would have an impact and a voice. That is the huge upside."

Summary

We found the students in both groups we interviewed to be much like their peers in other studies of the current generation of college students. They felt somewhat alienated from the way politics is practiced, but they did not have any deep sense that the system is fundamentally flawed. They were concerned about the lack of information they have about what is going on in government and they saw college as a time when they can acquire more of that information. On the other hand, they foresaw little likelihood of becoming politically engaged beyond the campus while in college. Instead, they spoke often of citizenship as something that was being deferred during this time. They imagined themselves to be citizens in the future (although even then some anticipate being too busy with other things), but as they began college they saw their main role as a "college student." Few of them imagined themselves doing anything they defined as "political" during their time in college.

There were some differences between the Democracy Fellows and their class cohort that bear mentioning. The Democracy Fellows, because they signed up for a program that involved a four-year commitment, understandably saw themselves as being more involved on campus than their peers. While all of the Democracy Fellows had at least *some* interest in politics, there were more comparison-group participants who had very little or none at all. Not only would the class cohort defer involvement during college, but many seemed likely to make that a permanent deferral. For these students, politics was a particular major or subject matter—such as biology or chemistry—and some people did it, enjoyed it, and were welcome to it. These students were the most likely to think that there was little that colleges could or should do to try to get students to be politically active.

The most interesting paradox is the finding that the students' own experiences in high school, and the models for civic education that they favored, seem to contradict their notion of how they anticipated spending their time while in college. Prior to college, they had learned most and became most interested in politics when they engaged in experiential learning through activities like debate and model UN, and the models they favored for civic education were clearly the more experiential ones. And yet, because they perceived so many competing claims on their time they were more likely to think that the traditional academic model was the means by which they would actually get most of their political knowledge. Furthermore, they tended to define the traditional model quite narrowly as political science courses. They did not visualize their entire college experience as a lesson in democratic learning and living, and, in fact, had a great deal of ambivalence about the model that imagines higher education operating in this way. Overall, they perceived their academic pursuits and their social lives in competition with learning citizenship, rather than as a means to that end.

Our data suggest that entering WFU college students expect to defer their citizenship during their college years. They view college as a "holding tank" of sorts, and when they leave it, they think they will be responsible citizens. The question for those concerned with civic education is this, what is it that students learn during this deferral time and what is the impact of that learning on the kind of citizens they are when they depart? It seems likely that learning that citizenship can be deferred for four years while one focuses on study and fun might well be a lesson that sticks when that individual enters the "real world." After all, there is even more "out there" that can preoccupy us and take precedence over public engagement; surely making a living and raising a family are at least as time consuming and attention grabbing as studying for tests, writing papers, and hanging out. If students instead can learn to practice citizenship skills in the college setting and thus increase their sense of efficacy as citizens engaged in a community, it seems likely that they will continue that practice when they leave college.

CHAPTER THREE

Deliberation in the Classroom

Chapter Three

Deliberation in the Classroom

I n our exploration of the potential contexts of civic education, we began our experimentation with deliberation in the classroom. Here, we asked ourselves whether the classroom is a microcosm of the larger political landscape or a venue for change. Is it possible to appropriate the best of deliberation, use it to teach students another means of political discourse, and allow it to work the "transformative" magic (Mathews 1998, 1999) which its advocates claim?

The available empirical evidence about teaching deliberation is sparse, but promising. In a study of adolescents in five countries, Hahn found that when students were exposed to classroom discussion of controversial issues, they were slightly more likely to develop attitudes that led to later political participation (1998, 233). Ervin, who tried to incorporate deliberation in her first-year writing course, found that there was little change in attitudes toward politics at the end of the semester (1997, 390). She did, however, find that "while thinking and expressing opinions in class might seem like rather benign forms of participation, students who engaged in them seemed to feel better equipped to move through their world actively—if not as *activists*, then at least as informed citizens" (1997, 391). Another study concluded that classroom deliberation exercises using the National Issues Forum (NIF) booklets have helped students gain a clearer understanding of political questions, become aware of possible answers, and see a connection to their lives (Reeher and Cammarano 1997). Finally, Doble, Peng, Frank, and Salim (1999) found that high-school students who had extended exposure to the NIF model gained new public knowledge, skills, and attitudes that they were then able to apply to new issue scenarios presented to them.

The important point of intersection between both defenders and detractors of deliberation, is that it is an "art," and as such, it "can be taught" (O'Connell and McKenzie 1995, 231). Furthermore, as Dryzek (2000, 169) argues, "the mechanisms endogenous to deliberation itself" are so compelling that it might be taught on its face as a valuable life skill, totally apart from its utility as a catalyst for responsible citizenship. Scholars, such as Gutmann, affirm deliberation's rehabilitative potential and argue that higher education is one of deliberation's best venues:

> Learning how to think carefully and critically about political problems, to articulate one's views and defend them before people with whom one disagrees is the form of moral education to which young adults are more receptive and for which universities are well suited (1987, 173).

In this chapter, we explore the advantages and challenges that are to be had in teaching deliberation skills in the classroom setting. We begin by sharing lessons learned from our prior experiences with teaching deliberative skills in other classes.

Group Decision Making Is Not Valued

Students arriving at college often take a dim view of group decision making. Despite their young age and limited experience, many students have negative attitudes about their previous group encounters. As have many other participants before them, they have found groups to be slow, often ill-informed, and uneven in participation (Beebe and Masterson 2000; Bormann 1996; Brilhart 1995; Gambetta 1998). Most prophetic of the growing decline in civic participation is the fact that students also fear that their individual interests will not be best served if left to the whims of collective decision making. Repeatedly, students express a profound sense of distrust and the need for what Hofstede terms *emotional independence* (1980, 221) from group decisions which might restrict their individual progress and success.

Given this negativism toward group process, it is not surprising that students' discussion skills are not well developed. They are comfortable and often skilled at monologue, but lack little sense of what it means to cooperate with others in public dialogue and group problem solving. Other scholars have attributed this interactional deficit to the "American emphasis on personal independence and individual uniqueness" (Rothwell 1998, 11; see also Samovar and Porter 1995) or what Barber (1984) terms the "American anarchist." Apparently when given a choice of communicative proficiencies, the rugged, individualistic Americans prefer to shore up their personal rhetorical skills rather than to learn the painstaking give-and-take of deliberating with others.

Deliberative Skills Do Not Come Naturally

Students must be taught to balance speaking and listening, and this balance must be reinforced by a skilled teacher or moderator (Ryfe 2006). Perhaps one of the most discouraging, "anti-democratic" findings of our experience is that individuals, even smart ones, can rarely be "turned loose" to deliberate and be expected to achieve a good result. What is "natural," or at least what we are socialized to do, is to present and defend our own points of view. One of the most consistent critiques of public talk and deliberation is that it can be dominated by those who are most articulate, knowledgeable, and comfortable with the public expression of their opinions. When this happens, the goal of finding real common ground is lost to a false consensus imposed by those with oratory skills (Gambetta 1998, 21). Despite our general commitment to participatory classrooms, the classroom dynamic often falls into the pattern seen so often in class and in politics: those with the strongest opinions and greatest rhetorical skills dominate the discussion. We have found that this problem can only be overcome through very intentional discussions linking the class dynamic to the broader theoretical issues we are discussing.

Knowledge Generated through Deliberation Is Expansive

One of the undisputed advantages of deliberation in all its venues is that knowledge of the issue is increased. Some worry about the quality of that knowledge or what citizens do with it once they have it, but even such detractors as Stokes (1998, 136) agree that "increasing the amount and variety of data that inform collective decisions" is one of deliberation's virtues.

All our previous deliberative class formats required a research component prior to deliberation, under the assumption that participants make better-informed decisions when they operate from a common baseline of shared information. Ostensibly there are no "experts"; all are offered an equal opportunity to approach the deliberation as well-informed participants.

What the students notice is that the knowledge shared through deliberation has a reflexive, synergistic quality. Because deliberation is "dynamic" and "active" as Dewey (1960) noted, it expands exponentially as it is shared and expanded upon by the group— as it is "socially constructed" rather than "received" (Osborn and Osborn 1991). So it does not escape students' notice that there is something qualitatively different about what they learn and retain from their deliberative experiences as opposed to the lecture formats to which they are most accustomed. Across semesters, class polls repeatedly demonstrated a clear preference for the deliberative format.

Intrinsic Interest Catalyzes Discussion

It has been argued that political alienation is fueled by a widespread disregard for what citizens hold important; as one UC-Berkley student told Harwood Group researchers studying college students' attitudes about politics: "I just don't think it's [politics] relevant for people like me" (1993, 19). Consistent with the wider polity, deliberations in our previous classes were dramatically affected by whether the students found the issue-at-hand relevant and important to them. The difference in energy and commitment between student-generated topics and mandated ones (no matter how salient the latter category might appear to an instructor) was palpable. Furthermore, as students grew increasingly comfortable speaking in the classes, they slowly moved toward linking deliberation and politics; they began to appropriate the discussion space in each class for their own pet political projects. These included issues like the campus alcohol policy, racial tension, and their own experiences with campus "democracy."

Diversity Complicates Deliberation

Students' greatest challenge in successful deliberation is in
entertaining diverse viewpoints and finding common ground
that includes everyone. One of deliberation's greatest challenges
is negotiating diversity—providing a space that accommodates
all players. Deliberative technicians, such as Habermas (1984)
and Benhabib (1996), argue that this accommodation is a must;
"difference democrats" recognize its difficulty. (See, for example,
Mouffe 1999; Young 1997.) On whichever side of this debate one
comes down, teachers of deliberation must find a way to manage
diversity. Indeed, in our experience, engaging the "other"—person,
race, fraternity, gender, political persuasion, personality, point of
view, social background—is the most difficult aspect of deliberative
training. As one Wake Forest student interviewed for the Harwood
Study (1993, 25) remarked: "The first time someone doesn't agree
with you, the last thing on your mind is looking at their point of
view." This intractability is especially troubling at Wake Forest
because our students are relatively homogeneous. Having similar
socioeconomic and cultural backgrounds and comparable deliberative capacity, they might have been expected to confront their
limited differences with relative ease. In fact, for the most part, they
preferred not to confront them at all. What we found in our classes
prior to the Deliberative Democracy seminar was that students had
a tendency toward premature agreement, which seeks to preserve
the peace and the illusion of harmony (Mutz 2006).

The "other" becomes especially problematic when the time comes
to find a resolution that includes minority opinions. Examples of
issues in which minority opinions have been marginalized and the
resolution hijacked are gay and lesbian rights, affirmative action, and
religious tolerance. Time and again the urge to force conformity
manifests itself in the wording of the resolution. Only the most
tenacious dissenters are represented in the final product; the more
fragile positions are coopted into strategically ambiguous language
(Eisenberg 1984) or simply fade away "as weaker people . . . sheepishly acquiesce to the stronger" (Gambetta 1998, 21). On the other

hand, classrooms where diversity is significant may well have the opposite problem: inability to come to any resolution at all (Ryfe 2006, 81; Shapiro 1999).

To respond to these problems we have used the techniques of monitoring the proceedings for exclusion (i.e., instituting ground rules for discussion that reinforce equity, urging students to take responsibility for their more reticent peers, and, as moderators, directly calling upon those students who are having difficulty entering the discussion); attempting to create an open classroom environment (i.e., utilizing a modified lecture—discussion format in which student's opinions are integral, continually reinforcing active listening, and providing numerous opportunities, both formal and informal, for feedback between students and to the professors); and beginning our first-year seminar deliberations with personal storytelling. All of these techniques are helpful but they have not eliminated the problem. Iris Young (1997, 399) offers some promising approaches: She would have us reframe difference—to see it and to teach it as an asset rather than a liability, as a "necessary resource for making the wisest and most just decisions." She contends that we need to learn to present but not objectify our individual "perspectives" when we enter the deliberative arena, to moderate the "I want this's" and "I want that's" of personal advocacy, and to appeal instead to one another on the basis of justice. Students of diverse backgrounds should be able to come to the deliberation believing that "I have the right for my perspective to be heard and the adding of my perspective to the collective repository will contribute to a better, wiser decision." Young argues that "dialogue across difference" allows students to learn to moderate their expressions of self-interest in favor of a sense of justice, to gain context for their own perspective in the light of the perspectives of others and to contribute to the collective repository of social knowledge. Enslin, Pendlebury, and Tjiattas (2001, 129) recommend Young's formulation to teachers of citizenship as a technique with "generosity of perspective." Ivie puts it even more succinctly when he suggests that teaching the ability to dialogue across difference might enable us to court "the internal Other sufficiently to reduce exaggerated fears of the external Other" (1998, 503).

Learning Is Developmental

Our thinking about civic education has also benefited from the work of John J. Patrick (2000), who, as we noted in a previous chapter, identifies four key components of effective civic education:

- the acquisition of *knowledge*;
- the formation of *cognitive skills*;
- the development of *participatory skills*; and
- the encouragement of *dispositions of citizenship*.

We were attracted to Patrick's framework because it provided a multi-tiered approach to understanding the goals of civic-engagement work and the foundational premise that such understanding is developmental, starting with basic skills and moving toward higher-level thinking. Our project had been designed similarly, starting in the classroom and moving out into the community, thereby taking into account the maturing, both educationally and politically, of our students.

Applying the Lessons

The first exposure to deliberation for the Democracy Fellows came through a first-year seminar during the fall of 2001. The group of 30 students was divided into two seminars that met at different times and were team-taught by the investigators. All first-year students at the university must enroll in a seminar of this type, and while subject matter varies widely, all seminars are expected to promote critical thinking through experiences in oral expression (i.e., group discussion, public address) and regular writing assignments.

Our seminar focused on the theory and practice of deliberation. (See Appendix A for the course syllabus.) We began by exploring democratic theory about the citizens' role in a democracy and the importance of public talk. We then taught the students how to deliberate through three deliberations in which we served as the moderators. We followed the NIF model for these deliberations (see Ryfe 2006, 93, for a detailed description of the NIF model), using NIF issue books that focused on public education, race and ethnic tensions, and the role of the university in promoting civic engagement. In this section of the class, we also talked about the lessons we had learned from previous experiences about the challenges of deliberation, and we encouraged the class to think about ways to overcome these challenges. After each deliberation, we spent time "debriefing," talking through what went well, what went less well, why these problems developed, and how they might be overcome. Finally, we taught the students how to frame an issue for deliberation, using their campus as the community to be studied (Kettering Foundation 2001). They worked in groups to investigate issues facing the campus that would lend themselves to deliberative discussion, worked through the process of selecting one of the issues, and finished the semester by framing the issue in a way that could be used to write an issue book (which they did the following semester as part of the Democracy Fellows program). (See Appendix B which offers a teaching outline for issue framing.)

At the end of the semester, the students were asked to write a final essay that examined their experiences with deliberation, the extent to which those experiences corresponded with the theoretical literature from the start of the class, and the prospects for deliberation as a method of developing citizenship both on college campuses and in the larger society. Our assessment of the impact of the seminar is based in part on these essays, as well as on our own observations, and the comments offered about the seminar in subsequent interviews with the fellows.

Evaluating the Classroom Context

It may go without saying that the classroom is an obvious context for teaching college students deliberation. At most institutions, the classroom and the curriculum represent the domain in which the faculty exercises primary control, offering the potential for the achievement of each of the educational components for effective civic education identified by Patrick. However, we found the classroom to be a stronger venue for teaching knowledge and critical thinking, than for simulating an actual political environment or for appreciating the dispositions of citizenship that reveal themselves when discussants are directly affected by the issue-at-hand. We consider the positives of the classroom venue first.

Acquiring knowledge. Consistent with Patrick's notion of the importance of political knowledge, we found in our early interviews with fellows and the class cohort that one of the significant and self-identified barriers to participation was a lack of knowledge and a lack of confidence in the knowledge they had about the political system, how it operates, and how they can be involved. We found in later interviews that a strong predictor of confidence in their ability to engage in politics was the classroom experience of learning about the political system and how it operates. We also found that whether students had acquired that knowledge often depended on whether they had sought it out in their course selection. Even with a broad, two-year liberal arts divisional curriculum, it was possible for students to avoid spending any time learning about politics.

Students who were not in the Democracy Fellows program were less likely to have had classroom exposure to discussions of democracy and citizenship, even after four years of college. Democracy Fellows, who went on to select a variety of majors, most of which were not political science or communication (our individual fields), nonetheless all shared at least the exposure obtained in the first-year seminar. One student wrote in his final first-year essay, "I have found in this short time span of the Deliberative Democracy class . . . that I learned more about the history of basic ideas about democracy than I have in the rest of my life." The fellows' enhanced confidence in their role as active citizens and their ability to talk knowledgeably and critically about deliberation, democracy, and citizenship were evident in each of the subsequent years of interviews following the first-year experience.

Linking theory and practice. Classroom deliberation enabled students to "enact" both the knowledge about political and deliberative theory they had learned and to practice it in ways that reinforce the cognitive skills and the political dispositions that Patrick recommends. Furthermore, the classroom offers a "safe" environment where the consequences of stumbling or erring are far less than they are in the "real" world. Practicing democratic skills, such as deliberation, in the classroom also allows students to become more analytical about the functions of public talk, for example, by engaging in it themselves and then stepping back and assessing what they have just experienced. Following each of our classroom deliberations, we asked the students to apply our theoretical discussions about the benefits and challenges of deliberation to the experience they had just had. These debriefing exercises were always the most insightful discussions of the class.

One such debriefing session in particular stands out. Our deliberation on race and ethnic tensions had been a difficult and often painful two days, and the fellows showed little ability at the end to find common ground. Our debriefing of that experience—Why was it so hard? What does that tell us about deliberation about difficult issues?—was one of the most powerful learning experiences of the class. Not only did the debriefing require keen and honest description, explanation, and evaluation of what had occurred, it brought students face-to-face with their own personal dispositional deficits where race is concerned.

Democracy Fellows talked about this deliberation quite a bit in their final essays as they processed what that experience might mean for the usefulness of deliberation. For example, one student left the class somewhat skeptical about its utility: "In our class with race and ethnic tensions," she wrote, "we were not able to talk through the issue. If only fourteen people of limited diversity of perspectives cannot talk through an issue and find common judgment, then I am skeptical of the ability of a larger group of people to deliberate." Furthermore, she noted the dispositional flaw that she had witnessed: "instead of meeting together at a common point, we went away from each other."

On the other hand, other students talked about how much they had learned from the experiences of hearing the perspectives of others who were different from them. In talking about the way in which group knowledge emerged through the deliberation, one student wrote, "I discovered this truth as I experienced my first deliberations. . . . When I entered a deliberation, I possessed a personal knowledge of the issue, yet by temporarily putting aside my view and listening to others' stories, I gained a public knowledge about racial and ethnic tensions and public education that I would never have had alone."

Transferring skills to other settings. Clearly, Patrick confined his recommendations of the four primary skill sets to civic education alone. Our students, however, were eager to extend the influence of their deliberative training. In their final essays for the seminar, they talked enthusiastically about how they might carry the skills into the rest of the college experience. One student, who had entered the program with a good deal of skepticism about politics, wrote:

> Though I cannot transform the political apathy of all of my peers, I must realize that the first step to political activism is a change of attitude. . . . Throughout the course . . . I have received the opportunity to realize how deliberation can transform an apathetic, disenchanted public into an active, engaged citizenry. The possibility of this vision truly excites me.

Another student wrote that her "role as a politically engaged citizen is vital to the success of this model." She went on to say that during the semester she had "come to appreciate" the deliberative democracy model, but that "for a more deliberative democracy to be established in America, I must do more than appreciate the model. I must promote it and commit myself to action on the decisions made in deliberations."

"One of the best ways I can demonstrate the effectiveness of deliberation to citizens," wrote another young man, "is to invite members of my community to participate in an actual forum that is of specific concern to them."

Some years later in our senior exit interviews, the Democracy Fellows talked about how learning the deliberative model for talk and embracing the democratic ideals underlying it had influenced the way they developed as students and as campus citizens. For example, one student said:

> I think the [skills of deliberation] will always be a consider-
> ation when I'm ever in a group. . . . I think that if I'm

> remotely in charge or have the ability to contribute to the manner in which . . . things are going, I would encourage [deliberation] because it's applicable to everything. Fraternity stuff, definitely. In the business world, yeah.

This same student described his use of deliberative skills in leading his fraternity during the senior year.

Other students talked about their use of these skills while serving, in one instance, as a resident advisor in the dormitory and even in their personal relationships with friends. Perhaps most significant, in terms of the impact on how we talk about and practice politics, students identified their experience with deliberation as having a current and future impact on "speaking with and listening to others," being "open-minded," and "taking seriously the other's point of view." While we made no specific attempt to tie the foundational knowledge, practice, cognitive development, and keener dispositions of the first-year seminar to their wider lives and practice, our students, almost to the last one, insisted on making that connection.

In short, classroom deliberation, yielded all of Patrick's civic-education guidelines. However, as later discussion will show, we regarded knowledge acquisition and cognitive development as the classroom's greatest victories; participation and development of political dispositions gained traction in the more authentic venues the students would later experience.

There were also limitations. Despite the obvious learning advantages of the classroom setting, we found that classrooms are unable to simulate an authentic democratic environment and discussion. Thus Patrick's criteria must of necessity be attenuated when: the classroom is more like a lab, than the "real world"; student "citizens" are not really in charge of their own destinies; and student deliberators have little power to move from talk to action. It is especially difficult to cultivate in student deliberators the political dispositions that come from deliberating alongside those citizens personally affected by an issue.

The undemocratic characteristics of the classroom. The classroom, with its teacher-student relationship, presents challenges to the democratic ideals of deliberation. The reality is that, in the classroom, students must be evaluated and graded and the persons responsible for that assessment are the professors. Thus, despite the effort to make the classroom as democratic as possible, in the end, the power imbalance remains. Even if we believe that grades are counterproductive, most of us are not at liberty to abandon them.

That reality creates an artificiality in the classroom exercise of practicing democracy, which is very difficult to overcome. In our own case, with so much class time given over to discussion, deliberation, and other forms of participation in the work of the class, we did not feel able to eliminate from these practices some kind of evaluation. Admittedly, we gave students frequent feedback and encouragement in one-on-one encounters to make that evaluation as educationally valuable as possible, but in the end, they were all aware that for the purposes of the class we, as instructors, were not their "fellow citizens." Classrooms are great settings for exposure to, and experimentation with, democratic ideals, but in the end they are not great models of democratic communities, in part because of the demands and expectations imposed upon them by the larger university structure.

Further, the classroom is not immune from the recurring democratic problem of individual dominance, especially if grade-motivated students believe their individual contributions are being assessed. There are several remedies for ameliorating this problem in the classroom (and possibly in public deliberation outside the classroom). First, skilled moderation seems essential to promoting dialogue that is productive and inclusive. Second, class exercises that focus on understanding and using the particular skills necessary for deliberation can be used. For example, in the first-year seminar we designed a workshop that specifically focused on practicing the skills of listening and of identifying the values underlying particular policy positions of others.

Despite our best efforts at being intentional about teaching the deliberative "rules of the game," designed to moderate the problems of power and dominance in the class, those problems were not eliminated. In reflecting on their classroom experience, some students saw the same unequal power dynamics at work that exist in the larger political realm. One young woman noted that in the class this dynamic "was fairly evident—at times only a few people talked and while the others may have had comments to make, the floor was controlled by a select few." Over time, however, there was a perception that in this regard, the group had improved. "Our third deliberation," wrote one young man "was marked by students engaging other students, and more participation by more people. Some of the earlier discussions had been heavily dominated by a few people whose views I do not think are representative of the group as a whole." Another rather quiet young woman became a believer in deliberation because, despite some ongoing power differential, she thought all voices had been valued and "everyone is allowed to participate." She wrote, "We see that deliberation does more than tolerate differences; it uses them."

The disconnect between the classroom and the real world. The insulated character of the classroom also seemed to undercut the possibility of transferring deliberation out into the world. Despite classroom opportunities to link theory and practice that appeared to teach that deliberation could "work" to reduce polarization and conflict over difficult public issues, the students were not altogether convinced.

In their final first-year essays they talked with optimism about the potential of deliberation in some essentially educational settings but with pessimism about the barriers to making it work in the larger political world. They recognized that citizens would have to be trained, as they had been, to think about politics differently, and they wondered about the willingness and the ability of people to take the time to learn to deliberate. One warned of the danger of holding deliberations without the "proper learned skills," and another lamented the fact that "most citizens lack the skills necessary to take part in constructive deliberation." For some of the students, the necessity of learning to "do deliberation" appeared to be an obstacle to its success in the broader community.

In later years, the Democracy Fellows even expressed skepticism about the prospects for a more democratic campus, pointing to the clash they identified between the ideals of democracy they had been exposed to in our class and the reality of what they encountered in other classrooms, in campus life, and in the broader political world. In their senior interviews, they still held on to the notions learned in the Deliberative Democracy seminar about what citizenship *could* be and the value of deliberative talk in their own lives, but they were also very much aware of the countercultural nature of the model and the challenges of implementing it in the real world. Clearly, the classroom setting cannot adequately simulate the challenges of implementing democratic practice in the world beyond it.

The difficulty of moving from talk to action. Finally, the deliberative model we employed in this project leads to an end point in which the group participants seek to identify common ground for action. Participants are led by the moderator to think about where they have found common ground in their discussion and what concrete actions they might take as individuals and as a group to bring about change in the policy area they have been discussing. Students in the seminar found this to be the most difficult part of the classroom deliberations on education and race, largely because they felt they had no power to influence policy outcomes regarding the issues we discussed. They were occasionally able to identify individual actions they could take—tutor a child in the local schools, try to get to know someone of a different race or ethnic background —but they were unable to think of themselves in a collective sense as having any power to influence education policy or racial and ethnic tensions.

When we talked with the students about their frustrations in coming to action, they identified their lack of power to influence decision makers. Their final essays reflected this frustration and their still fragile sense of efficacy. Reflecting on the class deliberations, one young woman wrote that "there were several issues [where] we, as students, felt that we had no control over the problem, and therefore had little motivation to act." Another student said, "When we deliberated on public education, although our discussion was enlightening, I did not feel fulfilled because we had not changed anything. As students, discussing an issue where the greatest change was needed at an institutional level, we felt powerless." Still another said simply, "The one thing that was lacking from our deliberative democracy class was the resolution of issues."

The role conflict for teachers.[9] The reality of evaluation requirements was only one of the challenges we faced as teachers of this class. One of the first challenges we encountered as we conducted forums in the classroom was the uncomfortable difference between moderating a forum and our traditional role of leading a discussion about readings and ideas introduced in class (Harriger and McMillan 2005). While we have both striven over the years to create free space for students to think and develop their own opinions, we have also seen our role as teachers as requiring guidance in steering students to wrestle with hard questions in our disciplines. Given that we had more substantive knowledge of the subject area, we felt free, as these discussions unfolded, to provide additional information, steer the students away from overgeneralizing from their own experiences, and move them toward larger abstract conclusions about the subject matter. In fact, we prided ourselves in our reputations as professors who encouraged and effectively guided discussions in the classroom. While we always tried, and usually succeeded, in keeping our personal views about issues out of the mix, we believed and acted on the belief that discussions would lead to particular conclusions corresponding to the theories of the disciplines we studied.

After we were trained in moderating deliberations and began moderating the classroom NIF deliberations, we found ourselves chafing under the requirements for effective moderation, particularly

---

[9] A published version of this argument can be found in Katy Harriger and Jill McMillan, "Public Scholarship and Role Conflict," *Higher Education Exchange* (May 2005).

the neutrality requirement and the need to fade into the background. Good moderators disappear, we learned. And yet we also felt we knew from years of classroom teaching that the teacher matters to the quality of the discussion. The push-and-pull between the roles of teacher and moderator proved especially difficult as our students floundered in the complex and challenging issues of racial and ethnic tensions. We felt as though we were abandoning our teaching responsibilities in this strange new role as "neutral" moderator. There was no substantive outcome toward which to guide them, just a process to "manage" while they provided the substance. Having learned the model well, our students expected our neutrality and called us on it when they perceived it to have been violated. This experience served as one more reminder of the challenges to creating democratic classrooms and the way in which our own training and practices work counter to that ideal.

Summary

Our past experience with teaching deliberation and our intensive focus on it in the Democracy Fellows' first-year seminar led us to conclude that there is much to be gained in using the classroom to teach deliberative skills. The classroom can be a "safe" environment for experimenting with an unfamiliar approach and building skills before they are tested with the public. It is a space that allows the moving back and forth between theoretical concepts and practice and the development of critical thinking skills that facilitate that movement. But because the classroom is a "safe" holding cell for students, it does not really mirror the real world of politics that students will encounter. Once democratic skills are developed, it is important to test them in that larger world, and as our students moved from the classroom to a wider world the challenges of using these newfound skills became progressively harder and more "real."

CHAPTER FOUR

The Campus Experiment

Chapter Four

The Campus Experiment

Having gained a solid foundation of deliberative theory plus important cognitive and practical skills needed to deliberate effectively, the Democracy Fellows were ready for forays into participation and civic learning that the world beyond the classroom could provide. As teachers and designers of the research project, we reasoned that the gentlest transition from the safety of the classroom would be to plan and conduct a deliberation in familiar surroundings with an issue of inherent interest to students and about which they had considerable knowledge (McMillan and Harriger 2002).

It may seem self-evident that the campus would constitute at least one of the social spaces most hospitable to experimenting with deliberative techniques, but that is not always the case. There are those who believe that the institution of higher education is not constituted philosophically to be a strong and legitimate deliberative venue. Others say that the campus climate is too full of distractions and disincentives to foster serious political discussion. These misgivings rarely center on the positive potential of deliberation, i.e., bolstering political awareness (Ervin 1997), increasing clarity about political issues (Gastil and Dillard 1999b), widening political application (Doble, Peng, Frank, and Salim 1999), overcoming political pessimism and cynicism (Barber 1984), or about the potential of deliberation to advance Patrick's (2000) civic-education skills. Rather there are persistent concerns about the campus environment as a venue for authentic civic debate, and the worry that a negative or hypocritical deliberation experience on campus might be worse than having no experience at all.

Some critics argue that colleges and universities are not particularly suited to model deliberative practice when what students and other community members see at work is the "hierarchical, patriarchal, plutocratic structures" of their own academic institutions (Becker and Cuoto 1996, 10). Unaccustomed to sharing decision making (Allan 1997), colleges often "announce" decisions made by faculty, deans, residence-life and housing administrators, and boards of trustees, rather than eliciting discussion about them. (See McMillan 2004; McMillan and Hyde 2000 for notable institutional exceptions.) Students are left in the dark as to the rationale for these decisions or the process that engendered them. While this traditional process of governance may be nothing more than committed administrators and boards of trustees taking their moral and fiduciary responsibilities seriously, it is not designed to bolster the fragile political efficacy of students looking for opportunities to participate.

Some commentators worry about the allegiance of critical campus citizens to a deliberative environment: faculty, who often are ambivalent about civic endeavors and, at the same time, overburdened and pressed for time with their own research and teaching (Levine 2003; Rice 1996); students who, given the press of social life, classes, and job preparation, may not be willing to commit to the rigors of deliberation (Brisbin and Hunter 2003); and parents, whose priorities may be better facilities, enhanced academics, and passports to good jobs for their children after graduation rather than "enlightened citizen" sons or daughters (Riesman 1980). Finally, all the deliberative democracy literature raises critical questions: When all is said and done, will campus deliberation make a difference? Will it change attitudes? Will it engender actions? Will it create strong, informed, robust citizens?

While there is little empirical evidence to answer those questions, in a recent study Mallory and Thomas (2003) recount some promising practices at colleges and universities across the country. For example, the University of New Hampshire and Manhattan College have implemented a study-circles-type process to deal with campus/community issues. Participants include faculty, students, and administrators, and while the process is somewhat experimental, they offer valuable examples of discussion as a mechanism for building trust and solving a wide variety of campus issues. The NIF model, the form of democratic dialogue utilized in our study, is being employed at Franklin Pierce College. The Center for Civic Life there works with campus constituencies to promote conversations on community and diversity issues, and those involved with the center report that campus culture has improved because of its presence. A number of other initiatives in campuswide dialogue are described in a text edited by David Schoem and Sylvia Hurtado (2002), *Intergroup Dialogue: Deliberative Democracy in School, College, Community, and Workplace.* A few colleges and universities (e.g.,The Ohio State University, the University of Pennsylvania, and Gulf Coast Community College) are on the leading edge of the institutional movement to adopt deliberation. Some, such as Wake Forest, are proceeding with smaller steps.

The Campus Deliberation at Wake Forest

During the final month of the first-year seminar, the Democracy Fellows worked in groups to identify issues that might lend themselves well to a campus deliberation. They heard from speakers and conducted independent research through archival work and interviews. In the end, they presented their findings to the group and voted on an issue. They chose to investigate what they perceived to be the lack of a sense of community on campus among diverse groups of students and between students, faculty, administration, and the city of Winston-Salem.

Though we as researchers and teachers distanced ourselves from the decision-making process involved in choosing the issue for campus deliberation, we breathed a sigh of relief at the students' choice because other issues on the table included constructing a parking deck, converting Reynolda Village, (a nearby, upscale shopping center) into a student hangout, and replacing the current food service. We were pleased that, without prompting, the students ultimately rediscovered their previous training about what makes an issue "frameable" for deliberation: 1) it is of broad concern to a community; 2) it presents choices, but no clearly "right" answer; 3) it depends on a wide range of people and groups for action; 4) it suggests new approaches; 5) it has not been publicly debated for different courses of action and long-term consequences; and 6) it offers the benefits of public judgment to officeholders and leaders (Kettering Foundation 2001, 17).

During the second semester of their first year, the Democracy Fellows researched the subject and worked to frame this issue into a format that would lend itself to deliberation. Their initial research convinced them that Wake Forest had an impoverished community spirit—that indeed there was a dearth of unifying symbols and collective rituals to unite the campus. Some blamed this on a limited social life, exacerbated by the physical isolation of the campus and the psychological separation of various groups and organizations. Others said that with all good colleges, as goes the intellectual climate of the campus so goes its communal spirit. Still others contended that campus community is only as strong as its altruism—that the way to shore up internal campus community is to reach outward and share the colleges' abundant gifts and talents with its host community.

Using the NIF issue books as a model, they developed three possible approaches to what was believed to be a less than vibrant campus community at Wake Forest: to create a more inclusive and varied social life on campus; to reinforce and extend the intellectual aspects of the classroom to wider, more accessible venues; and to commit the college to a more responsible civic partnership with the Winston-Salem community. In addition, students identified the arguments for and against each choice, specified the trade-offs of values associated with each, and offered possible action ideas for each approach. This issue-framing exercise, as time consuming and intellectually challenging as it was, proved to be a significant lynchpin in the project. We will return to it in a later discussion of our findings.

A smaller group of students took this material and wrote an issue book that they tested within the group, revised, and then published. Most of the editing and refinement of the issue book occurred over the summer.

When the Democracy Fellows arrived back on campus for the start of their sophomore year, about half of them were trained to be deliberation moderators, as their peers began to work feverishly on publicizing and recruiting for the event. The issue book was distributed to the participants who signed up for the deliberation.

On October 8, 2002, the big night finally arrived. Some 120 people—students, faculty, administration, and townspeople—gathered in Benson Student Center to deliberate "Building Community at Wake Forest." With the exception of a rocky check-in procedure, which was necessary to distribute participants into small groups, the event got off to a fine start and excitement was high. Following a plenary session in which the issue was introduced by three Democracy Fellows, the large group was broken into smaller groups, in which each constituency was represented; the groups were moderated by Democracy Fellows. Some fellows worked with video cameras to tape a few of the small group sessions; others served as troubleshooters and runners between groups.

During the deliberation, participants filled out pre- and post-forum surveys. We used the surveys to measure the effects of the deliberation on participants' attitudes about the issue and their preferences for the various alternatives that had been identified in the issue book. Later in the chapter, we will report those results.

In the weeks following the deliberation, Democracy Fellows collected and collated data from each small group and analyzed them for themes and major findings. A group of Democracy Fellows was assigned to write and distribute a report on the deliberation findings to each individual who had participated and to the campus press. We, in the meantime, were conducting focus groups and administering political participation surveys to the Democracy Fellows, the deliberation participants, and members of the sophomore cohort in order to further probe the deliberation experience,[10] and to assess the civic maturation of Democracy Fellows as compared to the students in the comparison group.

Deliberation Training Enhances Efficacy

Given the well-documented fact that college students feel little sense of political efficacy, by far the most encouraging result of bringing deliberative training to the campus was the empowerment of those students who experienced deliberation directly, in contrast to those who had not. While we noticed some deepening and strengthening of Patrick's four catalysts of civic education (2000), especially in the area of critical thinking, they paled by comparison to the pervasive sense of empowerment the students reported from this venue. We learned about this by contrasting data from

---

[10] The focus groups following the deliberation served two basic research purposes, allowing us to: 1) probe more deeply into the deliberative experience for the two groups who had attended—the Democracy Fellows and the deliberation participants; and 2) conduct our annual comparison between the Democracy Fellows and their cohort, this year (members of the sophomore class), as to how each group was progressing in civic learning and maturation. Thus we conducted nine focus groups: three with Democracy Fellows, three with deliberation participants, and three with the sophomore cohort. At the beginning of each focus group, we asked students to fill out a survey that measured their campus activities and asked about their attitudes regarding civic involvement, in order to assess differences among the three groups on attitudes and actions regarding participation in civic activities. Following the participation survey, there were some questions common to all three groups, but other sets that were unique to the particular group. For example, the Democracy Fellows and the deliberation participants were asked questions the sophomores were not asked because they had not participated in the deliberation experience. The Democracy Fellows and the sophomores were asked questions about their first-year experience as it related to encouragement toward civic engagement, questions we did not ask the deliberation participants because they represented all four classes. All three groups were asked questions about student voice and engagement on campus, and all three were given the same hypothetical issue at the end, designed to test their ability to apply principles of deliberation to a new situation.

focus groups with the Democracy Fellows, who had had consistent deliberative training since their arrival on campus, the deliberation participants, who had attended the campus deliberation, and the sophomore class cohort who had no exposure to deliberation; through a political participation survey given to all students in the study; and finally, through the outcomes of the formal campus deliberation.

In many ways the campus deliberation gave a tangible social presence to the work that the Democracy Fellows had been about since their arrival on campus, and, at least in their eyes, appeared to increase their general student efficacy fairly dramatically. When a student-initiated, student-led forum succeeded in gathering 120 individuals from the university's major constituencies and generating ideas that were eventually translated into administrative policy changes, the shift in power, at least for a time, did not go unnoticed.

Key administrative figures had attended the deliberation and others were brought into the campuswide discourse after the fact. The issue book and the subsequent report of the findings were the subject of more than one administrative retreat by campus decision makers, including the Board of Visitors who invited three Democracy Fellows to make a special presentation of the issue book and account of the campus deliberation. The Board of Trustees also learned of the campus deliberation and its outcomes, as did the Division of Student Life. Possibly the most sweeping effect was a reevaluation of the first-year orientation by the freshman orientation committee. Though not all of the action items resulting from the deliberation resonated well with campus administrators, the creation of an on-campus coffee house and a fairly substantial revamping of the orientation schedule and content indicated to students that they had been heard.

One Democracy Fellow offered:

> I think that the [deliberation] we did on campus worked
> very well in that regard [increasing efficacy]. . . . We got
> all these people to turn out, and I really feel like some
> of the things that student government and other student

organizations did coming out of that and some administrators did . . . were very powerful reasons for why
[deliberation] would work [in the future].

Another fellow said: "Just in student government and talking
with other administrators and having that opportunity to see where
actually [the deliberation] went was actually very impressive." In
short, while students could point to several past issues on campus
where they felt disenfranchised (see McMillan 2004), the discussion
on building community was not one of them.

During this time, we also gathered data from the class cohort—
both through focus groups and a participation survey—to determine
how their political development compared to that of the Democracy
Fellows. Both groups were alike in believing that students were
provided ample opportunity for involvement and volunteering,
but they differed in that the class cohort felt less encouraged in
classes and through the campus culture, which they termed as
"apathetic" toward being engaged politically. One sophomore
opined: "[T]here is never going to be a Kent State on this campus!"
Democracy Fellows departed from many of the dispirited students
in the class cohort, however, by seeing both the academic rigor
of "Work Forest" and the challenges of political engagement as
compelling. Both groups perceived some limitation to student
power and voice on campus, but Democracy Fellows were more
resourceful in imagining how to work around that constraint.

The participation survey given to all students this year revealed
that a large number of them participated in community service.
In our two groups of interest, the sophomore cohort had the
highest participation at 92 percent but the Democracy Fellows
were close behind with 89 percent participation in this area.
(See Table 2.) These results track findings in other studies across
the country that identify community service as an area in which
today's young people are more likely than their elders to be involved (Long 2002; Putnam 2000). Interestingly, the class cohort
members were also substantially more likely to be a member of
a Greek organization than were Democracy Fellows.

Table 2
Participation in Campus and Community Activities

Activity	Sophomore Cohort	Democracy Fellows
Volunteering	92%	89%
Greek Organization	42%	22%
Voted in State/ Federal Election	37%	52%
Joined Club	50%	78%
Voted in Campus Election	67%	74%
Read Campus Paper	75%	89%
Read Other Paper	62%	85%

Note: Given the size of the sample, statistical analysis of the significance of the differences is not warranted; instead in our discussion of the data we note simply when basic frequency and percentages indicate differences of more than 5 percent among the groups.

It is significant, however that the comparison group had lower levels of participation in a number of other more "political" categories when compared to the Democracy Fellows. Fewer of them had voted in the last state/federal election, had joined a club, had voted in the last campus election, had read the campus paper regularly, had read a paper with wider news coverage, or had written a letter to the editor of either a campus or other publication.

The "news" of the study's second year was the clearly enhanced student efficacy reflected by those students who had participated in the deliberation. However, when juxtaposed against a somewhat fragile sense of political power, which many students reported, and the ways in which they were actually spending their time, the efficacy engendered by the deliberation seemed something of an anomaly, albeit a welcome one.

Even Limited Exposure Makes a Difference

Focus group responses from students, other than the Democracy Fellows, who had participated in the campus deliberation on October 8 were highly illuminating. Participants were asked to reflect on the campus deliberation and to share their assessment of its value, its strengths and weaknesses, and its applicability to addressing other campus and wider community issues. Some of them had had substantial experience in campus life, having been involved with student government and other campus initiatives; others such as first-year students and graduate students who had earned their undergraduate degrees elsewhere had had virtually none. Only two had ever deliberated before. One had been in a pilot first-year seminar in the fall of 2000 and the other had attended NIF deliberations in his hometown.

Overall, it is clear that the deliberation participants were enthusiastic about the process. They recognized and appreciated the values of hearing diverse voices; the equality given the participants' voices despite their status differences on campus; the ground rules that encouraged listening and taking seriously the views of others rather than polarized debate; and the structure and common knowledge provided by the issue book. In some contrast to the Democracy Fellows, for whom the rationale and values of deliberation were more well established, the deliberation participants had a kind of wide-eyed wonder about the potential for a process that was largely very new to them:

> It was really good to see like a lot of students come out just because a lot of us have our own different areas and issues that we're part of. We don't necessarily come together on particular issues so I thought it was a good way to get students of various backgrounds together to talk about their own experiences on campus and how they see different things. I was very impressed with the city showing. In my group there was someone from the mayor's office and it was just a voice that I had never heard and a viewpoint that I think often goes unnoticed on campus.

> I think any time you come on equal terms and get as many different voices and opinions and really understand the

issues that are going on, then I think any time you can do that that it is really valuable. Otherwise, you are left to your own research, your own opinions, and everybody hasn't learned from everybody else.

On more controversial issues, maybe not even related to campus, but just social and political issues, I think this is really the perfect place for it [deliberation] because a lot of times when you're in a debate setting, things can get too heated. The two sides are too fully vested in their issues [whereas] the deliberation actually encourages listening.

These students also expressed optimism that the deliberation would lead to changes in the campus climate, both in terms of how others would respond and how they themselves would become involved:

For me it was like, it is more up to the individual students like myself . . . instead of like getting into a routine where you're just going about your business and about your social life with your head down and not really paying attention to what else is around you and the other people. It is actually like "pick your head up and pay attention to who is around you and be more inclusive and just be more engaging to everybody"; and I think when you do that then it is only a matter of time till people start reciprocating those actions and then all of a sudden, your network has just expanded so much more than you ever thought it would.

In sum, the experiences of the deliberation participants demonstrate that exposure to deliberative methods—even in a single ad hoc event—can have the effect of increasing students' optimism and sense of efficacy about affecting change on campus and in their communities.

Exposure to Deliberation Teaches Critical Thinking

Critical-thinking skills are sometimes difficult to pin down, but, as noted previously, Patrick (2000) has helped us in that regard by breaking down those cognitive skills that strengthen mental muscle where politics is concerned (i.e. identification, description, analysis, explanation, and evaluation). As researchers, we wondered how these skills were being affected, if at all, by deliberation training. The Democracy Fellows, who had considerably more exposure to the theory and practice of deliberation, demonstrated advanced mastery of critical thinking skills in a number of ways. Framing the issue for example, required: finding and sorting through data to distill three possible approaches to building community at Wake Forest; identifying the arguments for and against each choice; specifying the trade-offs of values associated with each; and, articulating possible action ideas for each approach. The showcasing of critical skills really came to the fore, however, in and around the campus deliberation and the focus groups that followed. While the Democracy Fellows shared the excitement of the deliberation participants they had a much more critical eye on the process. In particular, they were able to identify deliberative form and structure—where it worked and where it fell short; to gauge participation patterns and their impact; to critique their own performances as moderators and recorders; and to speculate about outcomes. For example, Democracy Fellows demonstrated that they understood the general concept of deliberation and its uniqueness as political discussion:

> We kind of had the idea that everyone had read the issue book when they got into the deliberation and that they knew what the issues were. But then some people came in and they already had things on their mind that they wanted to talk about. . . . I felt that in that sense it was a little bit unfocused and that probably was due to their lack of experience with deliberation.

Another fellow distinguished between random talk and the more orderly progression of deliberation:

> At first I was like, these guys [deliberation participants] are just kind of talking about specific ideas that they have instead of really getting into the deliberation about the different approaches, but then I remembered what it was like for us our first couple of deliberations; just how we had grown into that and so it made me realize it is not unusual the way it went.

Democracy Fellows also indicated that they understood the microprocesses of deliberation with regard to ensuring that no participant should be ignored or overpowered, that all voices should be heard. Said one student moderator: "Our group . . . had a good balance. We had a good mix of people and they all participated. . . . I think you're just going to have some good groups and some bad groups. It is just part of the process." Another fellow said:

I guess because we know how to deliberate more properly it was frustrating to watch them [participants] struggle with deliberation; it was kind of like throwing a kid in a pool, like kind of like flailing around . . . at least my group was kind of uneven.

And, one student identified the critical issue of power:

We had a bit of a balance of power issue. The provost was in our group and the SG [Student Government] president was in our group. They felt the need to introduce themselves. Even though we really didn't want them to use the titles, they slipped them in anyway. I had a little bit of a problem with that.

Displaying one of the most important markers of critical thinking, Democracy Fellows were able to analyze and evaluate their own performances. One student critiqued the skill levels of student moderators:

There were some times when the moderators were hesitant to lead too much. I don't know if this was just the combination of the fact that we were students and there were some adults in there or going with the fact that moderator training had been a month earlier.

Another recommended the value of a skilled recorder:

Most of the people in our group talked and had some really good things to say. My only concern is I think that whoever is going to be the recorder needs to be trained . . . because the people's voices need to be recorded correctly and it is not just something anyone can do.

One student moderator reflected on the moderator's task of staying focused and keeping the discussion on track:

> My group was incredible and the discussion was great. I thought everybody made great points. We got off on one tangent at one point but they kind of brought it back and I helped them with that; but it was so fascinating, I found myself lost in the discussion as the moderator. That is a good thing I think because it was really powerful what people were saying. . . . It really felt like a collegiate experience.

Finally, there were moments in the focus groups when the Democracy Fellows displayed advanced critical skills, which were surely derived from their deliberation training. In an attempt to assess the students' ability to apply the deliberative model in new settings, all three groups of students in the study (Democracy Fellows, deliberation participants, and members of the sophomore cohort) were given a hypothetical campus situation involving an honor code scandal and asked to consider, as a group, how the campus should respond.

Our hypothetical scenario incorporated some "framing" of the issue by suggesting that the campus debate seemed to center around three possibilities for explaining why the honor code was not working. Were academic expectations too high? Was the student hearing body too lenient? Should we abandon the honor code and monitor all exams? After the students heard the hypothetical, they were asked to advise the Vice President for Student Life on the best response to this controversy. How should the university go about addressing the problem? Should student government do anything? What? If the students got bogged down in arguing about the choices, we tried to steer them back with process type questions: What would be the best way to find out what people really think? How should decisions about reform be made? Who should make them? How should the school determine whether this is an isolated incident or a widespread problem? We suspected that the Democracy Fellows would think about deliberation as a method for bringing the campus together to discuss the issue and wondered whether it would occur to other deliberation participants. We assumed that the class cohort, having had no exposure to the process, would be least likely to consider this approach.

While some sophomores in the control group mentioned the possibility of dialogue of some sort, most focused on the issue of honor as largely an individual and personal matter and never were really able to think about the process issues. They wanted to talk about their own experiences with honor and what the administration should do to enforce the code. Two of three groups of deliberation participants did eventually discuss conducting a deliberation around the issue, but they too first focused on the personal and administrative responses.

The Democracy Fellows were also slow to arrive at deliberation as an approach, but, not surprisingly, when they got there, their assessments of its possibilities were keener. They talked about the degree to which the honor code scandal was a "frameable issue," "encompassed values," and "would be of interest to a large number of people." And these insights required no prompting but spilled out once they hit upon deliberation as a possible process for addressing the issue. They noted, for example, that deliberation could be an effective means of gathering more information, determining the extent of the problem, and involving people across the campus:

> [The honor system] is based on trust. The thing that makes it work is the students who believe in it and follow it. . . . I think the discussion-based thing is a better way to go about it because then you know if cheating is more indicative of things going on or if these are really a couple of bad apples.

> This topic obviously promotes discussion. It is a great topic for discussion. Everybody has an opinion on it because it affects everybody.

> The main thing is getting new and fresh voices as opposed to having these people in student government and the honor and ethics council . . . like sort of the average student. You need to get the people that are sitting in their dorm right now playing video games.

In summary, Patrick's argument that cognitive development is an essential element of effective civic education clearly recommends the experience of campus deliberators at Wake Forest.

Altering Attitudes and Facilitating Action

The data from the pre- and postsurveys indicate that the deliberation did appear to alter the views and attitudes of many participants. The surveys showed that, in the course of the discussion, there was movement toward agreement that the issue as laid out in the issue book, was indeed problematic. Agreement increased by about 20 percent that the isolation of students from the wider community, lack of school spirit, and separation of campus groups were matters of concern.

Concern about these problems increased as the discussion progressed. The Wake Forest "bubble" which isolates students from the city, and the somewhat anemic school spirit, initially rated as "Very" and "Somewhat Troubling," became more so by 13.5 percent as the discussion progressed.

Just as important as the numerical findings were the open-ended responses in which a majority reported that the deliberation had altered their attitudes about community. Some were "more encouraged"; saw the "other" (professor, student, administrator, townsperson) as interested and caring; became more "open-minded"; learned more about the issue; and realized the issue was "serious." With regard to potential future action, most said they saw things they could do about the problem and were willing to try (i.e., meet more people on campus; go downtown and organize a senior walk; work on developing new traditions; promote events; get involved; work to change the WFU first-year orientation; and encourage others to participate). One student participant summed up the attitude change:

> I felt encouraged to be more active. . . . This [the deliberation experience] strongly encouraged me to do things through my organization. . . . There were issues that we were concerned about but we didn't know if everybody necessarily wanted them, but hearing what everyone said, faculty, students, city leaders, they were all on the same page.

Another deliberation participant foreshadowed the actions which ultimately took place in the weeks and months ahead: "I think students will do things. I think the student organization leaders who were there, especially after the results are published, will do things with the results." And indeed that is what happened. Not only did students begin to discuss and enact suggestions from the deliberation, but, as noted earlier, members of the administration and the student-life department took note as well.

The Campus Venue Presents Challenges

While we have reported many positive aspects of campus deliberation, this venue has its challenges: the familiar surroundings of campus life which rarely constitute a natural civic venue; limited issues that students actually have the ability to affect; and generally, the uneven playing field of campus power and governance.

Try as we might to simulate a natural, decision-making civic environment, remnants of the somewhat homogeneous and insulated bubble in which students live on campus remained. Though the issue book addressed a more thorough integration with the Winston-Salem community, the deliberation was still held on campus and attended mostly by campus citizens. Democracy Fellows still operated within their comfort zones as they made contacts, recruited, negotiated, and publicized. More important, the preponderance of the issues deliberated that evening kept students firmly in the center of their own narrow, self-interested universe—a situation that was to change dramatically when they took their deliberative efforts out into the wider Winston-Salem community.

A key component to successful deliberation is its ability to empower citizens to action—to enhance their participation in their own governance. While some believe that the limited role of students in campus governance should be reexamined (Allan 1997; Becker and Cuoto 1996; McMillan and Cheney 1996; Pernal 1977; Sullivan 2000), the current political status of most college students is one of transience and subjection to the quasi-parental oversight of the college they attend. That being the case, colleges and universities that want to engage in serious deliberation— certainly about campus issues—may experience some difficulty finding issues on which students can actually have an impact. We were fortunate that our students located such an issue.

Over the four years of our study we repeatedly asked students what role the university should play in learning to engage in citizenship. Most echoed the opinion of one WFU student who believes that students lack the maturity, experience, and commitment to participate in governance: "[I] don't think students should be elevated to be making major administrative decisions when there are people who are there in those positions for a reason." Another student feared that, if given equal authority for their own governance, students might show up to deliberate "only if there were free food." This is not to say, however, that the scope of student involvement cannot be enlarged, as indeed it was in the deliberation. The challenge for serious campus deliberations is to find issues on which students have the possibility of creating action—of actually contributing to an important outcome, lest the deliberation experience leave them further disillusioned about the promise of deliberative democracy.

Finally, the success of campus deliberation—at least in the minds of the students—seems clearly to rise and fall on administrative interest and response. During the four years of the study, students were consistent in identifying Reynolda Hall—the administrative building on campus—as the source of campus power. As with most top-down configurations in organizational life, it is also the case that if administrators do not get on board with some student initiative, it will most likely fail. Once again, in our case, the presence of some key administrators at the deliberation and the attention of others to its aftermath worked to level the playing field for the Democracy Fellows.

From Patrick's (2000) perspective, deliberation participants at Wake Forest vastly improved their political knowledge about a campus issue, reinforced both their cognitive and participation skills in a public venue, and strengthened their democratic dispositions—at least local ones—as they heard the viewpoints and perspectives of their fellow campus citizens. By far the strongest finding in and around the campus deliberation, however, had to do with student efficacy, which manifested itself in both attitudes and actions. Especially for the Democracy Fellows, their deliberation training seemed to have enriched the value of their academic lives; abated their cynicism; emboldened them to talk with peers and even superiors about politics; and empowered them to initiate influence attempts with the movers and shakers of their organizations, despite status. Deliberation training seems to have sparked more civic action as well.

CHAPTER FIVE

Deliberation "On the Road"

Chapter Five

Deliberation "On the Road"

If the campus deliberation allowed students to stay safely inside their bubble, the community deliberation clearly burst it, forcing them outside the protection of their teachers and friends and into the local community that surrounded them. Here they had to participate face-to-face with people often very unlike themselves and deal with hard, often intractable, issues that stretched students' minds by their complexity. And the literature would have predicted the students' discomfort. Murphy (2004) argues that despite the benefits of classroom and campus deliberation, there is a laboratory-like, unrealistic quality to them which fails to account for the "wrangle" (Burke 1969) which characterizes political discourse in the public sphere. To experience that wrangle and in particular to enhance their long-term commitment to civic engagement (Battistoni 1997; Boyte 1993; Rimmerman 1997), students must be given opportunities to experience deliberation in the communities where they live, or as Mitchell (1998, 42) puts it: to leave the "pedagogical bullpen, a peripheral space marked off from the field of social action," and to enter the game itself.

There is also the question of the institution's responsibility to the community around it. As the deliberative democracy movement gains traction, there is an increasingly plaintive cry which Thomas (2003) gives voice to: "Where are the colleges and universities?" There is growing discontent with the propensity of higher education to sequester itself from the messiness of public life, the confusion of critical policy issues, and from partnering with other institutions to solve the dilemmas of contemporary life. In this chapter we will examine the problems and the promises of such a college/community partnership.

Forging a Campus/Community Partnership

The problems. Though this picture is clearly changing with the increase of service-learning programs, for example, the record of higher education as a civic actor does not reflect a stellar performance. Bringle, Games, and Malloy (1999, 9) argue that there have been too many instances where institutions of higher education treat communities as "pockets of needs, laboratories for experimentation, or passive recipients of expertise," rather than as equal partners in tackling social and political issues that define their common existence. Brisbin and Hunter (2003) echo the complaint of many community leaders that colleges and universities often exude a certain arrogance that "objectifies" the community, except in those situations when the college needs something that the community has or when it is otherwise politically expedient. A kinder interpretation of this distancing of higher education is that the institution itself is constituted to operate according to the "charity" model where resources and surplus are transferred from one group to another (usually from "expert" academics to those in need of their expertise), as opposed to the "justice" model where resources are considered as property of the whole community and shared by all (Morton 1995).

Students also come in for their fair share of criticism with regard to the problems of college/community partnerships. In a 2001 study of civic leaders, business people, public educators, nonprofit workers, and students, Brisbin and Hunter found that students often have no powerful incentive to help people in a region where they are attending college. They see themselves as transient (Allan 1997; Becker and Cuoto 1996; McMillan 2004; McMillan and Cheney 1996) and therefore unwilling to make much commitment of time and energy to their host communities. Students tend to place classes, social life, and jobs ahead of civic engagement. On the other hand, those who do volunteer may do so not for altruistic or even pedagogical reasons, but because it will "look good on their résumés." While many student volunteers and interns have good attitudes, are eager to contribute, and want to learn, some only "show up" for the service requirement and "just try to get through"(Brisbin and Hunter 2003, 478), making them only marginally helpful in a constructive partnership. So while there are structural and attitudinal barriers to healthy campus/community relationships, or what many have come to call the "town/gown divide," there is also room for optimism.

The promises. Perhaps the most popular attempt at campus/community partnership has come in the form of service learning, which has mushroomed in this country over the past decade and a half. In this course-based, credit-bearing experience, students participate in a service activity that meets identified community needs under the direction of a classroom teacher who is tying the service to course content and to a general enhancement of civic responsibility (Bringle and Hatcher 2002). Educators see service learning as a way to introduce students to civic engagement without relinquishing the core academic component with which the service is connected (Enos and Troppe 1996; Eyler and Giles 1999; Morton 1996). Communities regard it as meeting a critical "need" for help, exacerbated by the declining participation of their citizens (Putnam 2000). Zlotkowski (1996, 1999) cites the significance of the service-learning movement as a transition toward healthier and more beneficial college/community partnerships.

Given our interest in deliberation, we also wondered how colleges were doing in "speaking with" and "listening to" their local communities. While relatively few colleges have chosen to become deliberative catalysts, Murphy (2004, 86) reminds us that there have been some efforts "to expand academic debate into community settings and to utilize local community issues" to engender discussion and to advance local participation. Mitchell (1998) argues for the concept of "argumentative agency," in which student debaters strengthen their democratic sensibilities by engaging community leaders, social movements, activist groups, and other groups typically excluded from traditional deliberations. The George Soros-sponsored Open Society offers a similar deliberative opportunity to disadvantaged populations (Murphy 2004). W. Barnett Pearce's (1998) Public Dialogue Consortium seeks to establish dialogue within and among groups in local communities, but to avoid the confrontational and adversarial climate to which many such efforts have fallen prey.

In short, many colleges and universities have been slow to initiate the conversation between themselves and their host communities (Thomas 2003). When academics do offer aid, it is often with the voice of the expert and not as a partner (Morton 1995). What colleges have been more willing to do, with some qualifications, is to offer up their students to engage the community with measured degrees of public service. The community deliberation planned and executed by the Democracy Fellows for the city of Winston-Salem was one such act of public service.

The Community Deliberation in Winston-Salem

Preparation for the fall community deliberation began in earnest in the spring semester of 2003. After some preliminary research, which identified the local problem of urban sprawl, the Democracy Fellows, and we as their mentors, realized that there was much about this issue that we did not know. We planned a campus dinner to bring together the fellows and key community leaders who represented critical areas of the issue. The purpose of the event was to hear the perspectives of diverse constituencies; to allow the fellows to question and to clarify their understanding; and to seek assistance in charting a research plan that would lead students to the best information on the subject and to wisely craft their issue book in advance of the deliberation. The positive response that we got to these invitations demonstrated the first bit of evidence that community leaders were eager to help. At the dinner, the fellows were able to hear from the mayor of the city, the head of the city/county planning office, a representative of the Sierra Club, a realtor and former alderman, the president of the Chamber of Commerce, and a member of one of the city's strongest neighborhood associations. Guests presented their perspectives, fielded the students' questions, interacted with one another, and offered advice as to where students should go next in their research and issue book preparation.

After several weeks of research, a small group of students began to construct the issue book. While the issue book for campus deliberation had been completely custom-made, for the community deliberation, students received permission to adapt an existing NIF book, *A Nice Place to Live: Creating Communities, Fighting Sprawl* (1999), which addressed the topic on a national level. Into that NIF framework, students inserted local facts, figures, and analysis to construct the issue book entitled: *A Place to Call Home: Building Communities and Smart Growth in the Triad*. Over the summer, the issue book was edited numerous times.

When students returned to campus for the fall semester of their junior year, planning began in earnest with a kick-off dinner meeting in which the Democracy Fellows were divided into four basic committees: recruitment, publicity, moderating, and logistics— categories that students knew well from their campus deliberation experience. Recruiting of participants began shortly thereafter; the issue book was printed and distributed; moderators underwent refresher training; and final logistical preparations were made for the event.

On October 2, 2003, the community deliberation on the subject of urban sprawl in Winston-Salem was held at SCIWORKS, a community science museum, and was attended by approximately 50 people. After a welcome and a short film on urban sprawl, attendees were broken into four groups, moderated, recorded, and timed by Democracy Fellows. Following the discussion, action ideas from each of the four discussion groups were pasted on the cafeteria walls at SCIWORKS, as participants enjoyed refreshments, reviewed results, and continued to converse about what had happened in their groups.

In the weeks following the deliberation, students sought to assess the proceedings and to construct a report of findings, which later was distributed to all participants and the local press. As researchers, our data gathering commenced as it had following the campus deliberation. Though we lacked access to the community members who had attended, we conducted focus groups with the Democracy Fellows to probe their attitudes about the experience.

As we will chronicle below, it was not the event that the students had anticipated nor that their campus experience had prepared them for.

Patrick (2000) suggests that civic learning falls short if students do not ultimately test their knowledge and cognitive skills by participating and developing political dispositions in the real world with real issues experienced by real people. The community deliberation on urban sprawl clearly offered such an opportunity. In fact, Democracy Fellows were clear that the infamous Wake Forest bubble was punctured, if not destroyed altogether, by what happened to them at SCIWORKS on that October evening. It was a bittersweet experience, in that both the students and we could clearly identify both positive and negative outcomes.

Early in this study, Democracy Fellows had a sense that the homogeneity of their campus was not a true test of the principles of deliberative democracy. Somehow students "got it" that there was a wide world just outside the campus gates inhabited by people with different points of view, habits, cultures, motivations and certainly political predispositions. In fact, even in the spring semester of their first year, they wrote in the issue book for their campus deliberation:

> Wake Forest University truly is its own little universe. A recent study published in the *Winston-Salem Journal* suggests that a student very well could, and many do, spend four years on campus and never once venture into Winston-Salem. All meals can be purchased on campus; there are cultural events, concerts, plays, religious services, parties, and sporting events, all tucked away into an isolated campus. Students at Wake Forest constantly comment on "the bubble" surrounding their campus. . . . This physical and mental isolation leads Wake Forest students to be unaware of and apathetic toward current events and social problems, especially at the local level (Democracy Fellows 2002, 9).

Repeatedly, in their interviews and focus groups, students had mentioned the need for diverse perspectives and pointed to having to leave campus to find them (i.e., in study-abroad experiences, visits to other campuses, and so on). However, when directly confronted with the prospect of dealing with citizens beyond the campus gates—the need to "write to *them*" in the issue book; approach *them* about the possibilities of a community deliberation; provide adequate motivation to coax *them* to attend; and deal with *them* in the sometimes tense and fractious moments of the deliberation—students found the diversity of democracy daunting. Still in all, there is little doubt that bursting the bubble was clearly this venue's greatest effect. Students also were able to identify other, more specific outcomes that characterized the experience.

Writing the Issue Book

In creating the issue book on local urban sprawl, students encountered two of Patrick's elements of civic education: the enhancement of cognitive skills and the advancement of democratic dispositions. This experience in issue framing was totally different from their previous experience in researching and writing about a problem in and around their own campus community, and they developed their critical thinking skills in an entirely different way. Despite the fact that students had received permission to use an NIF issue book on urban sprawl to structure their inquiry, they found their unfamiliarity with the subject, both nationally and locally, to be daunting. What they had learned in their classrooms and textbooks about the problem now had to be examined and tested against a unique set of circumstances in Winston-Salem, North Carolina.

Utilizing the orientation, advice, and networks of the local leaders who had attended the kick-off dinner, the Democracy Fellows set out in earnest to gather facts and opinions on their own. This research effort, which lasted several weeks, led students to the halls of local government, newspaper archives, developers' offices, and conversations with ordinary citizens. They also drove around the area to photograph the most crowded local strips of public highway. All the information was gathered and turned over to student writers who began to frame the issue book around three choices: shoring up suburban living, revitalizing the downtown area, and allowing the growth of the city to proceed without restriction. Every single one of Patrick's cognitive skills (identifying, describing, analyzing, explaining, evaluating, and thinking critically and constructively) was necessary to process the vast amount of information and to frame it in terms of national trends, while reflecting the unique issues and concerns of the local community. This research and the ultimate write-up taught them the particular problems that Winston-Salem faces and underscored the complexity of the issue for the average citizen.

Bridging the Town/Gown Divide

Patrick advocates student experiences that build democratic dispositions (e.g., taking up causes that promote the general welfare, that note our common humanity, and that support democratic principles and practices). As we noted at the beginning of this chapter, apparently many community leaders see the need for these dispositions as well. The deliberation appeared to bridge the town/gown divide for the Democracy Fellows, who gained a new appreciation for their adopted city, and received some appreciation in return from the citizens gathered on October 2. Students were encouraged that participants seemed to have read the issue book in advance and had come prepared to discuss it. Though initially, the fellows had neither known nor cared much about the issue of sprawl in Winston-Salem, the response of participants indicated that in their write-up of the issue of local urban sprawl, the students had represented accurately and fairly the problems that the city faces. For the students, this was a victory in and of itself. One student remarked:

> I think people that read the issue book were inspired by it because everyone that came, at least in my group, was very informed; you could tell that they had read the book. . . . And in general I think they were impressed with the book and very receptive to it.

For the most part, students also believed that the discussion had been a meaningful experience for those who attended. One student said that the smaller-than-hoped-for turnout (which we will discuss later) allowed for small deliberative groups, and he felt that improved the quality of the discussion:

> I don't think it would have been the same sort of dynamic within the group [with more people] . . . because the people who participated really enjoyed it and they felt it had been a worthwhile experience. I think we could see that afterwards when people were actually talking and mingling and looking at sheets on the board [other groups' notes].

Other students believed that participants left with more knowledge about the issue and about the views of people different from themselves. Some talked about participants seeing things in a new light or acknowledging that someone with whom they had disagreed actually had a good idea.

Many of the students also felt that their own viewpoints had been broadened by the deliberation. One Democracy Fellow noted, and others agreed, that:

> I learned a great deal from just hearing people from Winston-Salem who are not connected to Wake Forest. . . . The majority came from Winston-Salem without a connection to the university, and just being able to get different people together and listen to them talk about an issue that the majority of them felt pretty passionate about.

Some students reported that after the deliberation, they felt more adventuresome about exploring the city and interacting with locals. Clearly then, the students could point to many aspects of their first community deliberation that went right. Their positive assessment of the event was qualified, however, by the ways the experience left them feeling frustrated and disempowered.

The Difficulties of Community Organizing

The students seemed to have been particularly blindsided by the logistical aspects of community organizing, such as recruitment and publicity. Because the process of planning and implementing the forum on campus had proceeded with relative ease, students seemed surprised by, and unprepared for, the problems of dealing with people whom they did not know and whose particular constraints they were unable to appreciate.

Clearly, the central criticism the Democracy Fellows had of their community deliberation experience was their lack of success in getting a large and representative sample of the community to participate in the deliberation. Most disappointing was the response or lack of it from potential minority participants and their limited success in luring their fellow students off campus to attend. Those who did participate tended to be white, affluent, and highly educated. While there was some acknowledgement by the students of their own inexperience at recruiting for a sizeable event such as this, they focused their comments primarily on external constraints.

One student noted, with considerable agreement from others, that "It was an uphill battle . . . that we were losing from the very beginning because it's very difficult to get people to get involved in civil and government type issues. . . . It's like people just . . . go home, they're tired and just want to watch TV, that's it." Another student acknowledged that what they considered to be poor attendance "was partly our fault," but went on to say that "there was like no incentive for these people to come. . . . It is going to be hard to recruit people who just aren't interested and who don't have the time in their daily lives."

One student suggested that they may have taken the wrong approach to the second deliberation. "We kind of thought . . . since the first one went so well it will be so easy, we don't have to worry about recruiting, it should be easier. . . . We didn't realize that it was going to be actually a lot harder."

Many of the Democracy Fellows wondered whether the issue itself contributed to low turnout. While there have been problems of urban sprawl in Winston-Salem, and the region was recently identified in a national survey as one of the worst places for urban sprawl in the country, students felt that the issue may not have been sufficiently timely. (Earlier in the year a battle had been waged to annex a suburb to the city proper, but it was largely over by the time the deliberation was held.) Students also speculated that the public may simply feel that sprawl is an inevitable part of urban life and that there is little that could be done about it. Others mentioned the complexity of the issue and the knowledge required to understand it as factors that might limit broad-based participation in such a discussion.

Finally, students pointed out that the complexity of the issue also made more challenging the traditional discussion of courses of action at the conclusion of the forum. As one student put it, "It's such a monumental issue, it's almost like what can you do? Like what can one voice really change?" Another student said, "Sprawl is there; it's not like you're gonna take it away overnight or anything like that. . . . I think most people felt a little more helpless with urban sprawl." Also the presence of a city councilman who effectively "hijacked" one group discussion convinced students that while citizens may be heard in one evening's deliberation, real systemic change may happen only at the higher reaches of government.

It is interesting to note that the obstacles the students identified as hampering their efforts to engage citizens are common the world over to efforts to entice people into the civic arena. For students to truly learn about civic activism, perhaps the difficulties our students experienced in taking deliberation "on the road," may have been a decided value.

Limitations in Student Efficacy

Particularly troubling on October 2 was the Democracy Fellows widespread perception that they were inadequate and lacked credibility with the larger community. Students consistently mentioned their feeling that the community did not take them seriously as affecting everything from their ability to recruit, their comfort in even *trying* to recruit, and their credibility as moderators of the event. One student said, "I don't think people at Wake feel any connection to the town and I think a lot of people feel that the town doesn't like them, you know, that we're kind of like a burden to the town." Another student said it was "difficult for college kids to . . . get involved in the immediate community around them . . . especially maybe at Wake Forest, it is kind of hard to be taken seriously by the greater Winston-Salem community, maybe because most of us aren't from here and we aren't really all that acclimated." There was also discussion about the stereotype of college students in the community and how it may have affected the deliberation.

Finally, there was the matter of what students came to call the "hijacked" group. Among the four small groups that deliberated, one in particular stood out for the students because it highlighted the difficulty of power relationships in the deliberation process. This group contained an avowedly pro-business city councilman whose participation unfolded in problematic ways: First, he tended to assert his authority as someone who had insider knowledge of how decisions about economic development and growth were made; and second, his position tended to act as a lightning rod for those in the group who objected to the pro-growth policies of the current city council. Consequently, the deliberation turned into a debate between the city councilman and several community participants rather than a deliberation around the three choices presented in the issue book. The student moderator struggled to keep the group on track and others in the group (especially the students) appeared to resent the direction the discussion had taken, but once the pattern was set, it persisted. In hindsight, the hijacked group became a symbol for the students' feelings of political impotence—sentiments that shared space in their minds with feelings of satisfaction about the positive outcomes of the event.

A Different Kind of Community Deliberation Experience

It is instructive here to take a short detour and talk about a smaller group of Democracy Fellows who had an experience with deliberative practice in the community quite different from the one described above. Only one week after the community forum in Winston-Salem, they were invited to be moderators for a forum sponsored by the North Carolina Civic Education Consortium (NCCEC), a statewide organization whose focus is on improving K-12 civic education and to which one of the investigators belongs. The participants in the second deliberative exercise were high-school students, social-studies teachers, some education administrators, some representatives of local nonprofits and foundations, and local public officials from two adjoining counties. The conveners of the forum were eager to have college students play a role as moderators because they would provide a powerful example of youth engagement to the participants. All the Democracy Fellows were offered the opportunity to participate, and eight of them agreed to do so.

We met with the conveners of the forum for an hour prior to the event to go over what should happen in the small groups. After a presentation of data on youth civic engagement in North Carolina, the audience was broken into small groups to discuss the barriers to youth civic engagement and to generate action ideas for how communities and schools could overcome those barriers. The Democracy Fellows moderated these small groups, and during our focus groups, the students who had participated in this forum used it often as an example of a positive community experience.

For one thing, students in the NCCEC forum felt that the issue was one that lent itself to easy deliberation, both because it was generally uncontroversial and because the audience was already committed to improving civic education. Additionally, the students saw the issue as lending itself well to a discussion of action, partly because of the common ground and partly because the people who were there were people who could make these changes happen. This made the moderators' jobs easier and contributed to a general sense of good feeling that emerged from the discussions.

In contrast to their self-effacing assessment following the urban sprawl experience, the students in the NCCEC forum used the language of success and accomplishment in talking about this experience. Their expressions of efficacy seemed to be partly related to the issue itself (one that they were very familiar with because of their first-year seminar classroom experience and their own personal experiences as young people) and partly related to the positive reinforcement they received from forum organizers. They were recognized in the program, publicly acknowledged and praised *prior* to the small groups, and thanked profusely afterward for their contribution. As a result they appeared to feel more confidence and legitimacy going into the small groups and in assessing their contribution afterward.

An Ethical Dilemma

While both researchers appreciate the sometimes controversial discussion surrounding "engaged scholarship" or "public scholarship," we had regarded it largely as a nonissue. Particularly at Wake Forest, which espouses the "teacher/scholar ideal," we are expected to be good teachers, and it is assumed that teaching is routinely informed and enriched by whatever research we are engaged in. Furthermore, if that research is substantial, its focus is rarely questioned. In short, in our almost 50 years of combined experience, teaching and research have existed in a comfortable symbiosis. The community deliberation at SCIWORKS was to change that.

The most serious philosophical challenge presented itself both to our students and to us as teachers and researchers when we faced the tension between the value of the community deliberation as a pedagogical exercise and its civic value to the citizens and community of Winston-Salem. In our traditional faculty roles we felt the obligation to make certain that our students came away from the experience having learned more about deliberation and about how it might work in a large, diverse, political community. Consequently, we felt it was important for them to be responsible for organizing the event, recruiting the participants, and preparing the materials to be used.

Our tension came into sharp relief, however, when we watched the students underestimate the timing and complexity of advertising and recruiting for this event. If they did not do an effective job in these tasks, our teaching and research interests told us that it was best to let them "fail," given our belief that most learning comes from trial and error, and often, failure. But as citizens of the community, we felt an ethical obligation not to treat our neighbors as subjects to be experimented upon for our pedagogical and research purposes. We also believed it was important for the students to see that detachment was inappropriate. It would be wrong to invite community members into a public dialogue about making Winston-Salem a better place to live without doing our best to make sure that the experience was a positive one, at least in its execution, if not in its outcomes. In short, we came face-to-face with what it means when the community itself becomes the learning environment.

We ultimately decided to split the difference: convening latent committees, recruiting some friends and acquaintances, and shoring up flagging student spirits. We wondered, however, and continue to do so, if our decisions were the right ones, either for our student charges or for the people gathered at SCIWORKS that evening, who represent the community of which we are both a part. (See also Challenger 2004.)

In some senses, because of the nature of this project, students have been "under the microscope" from its inception. In another venue we have written about the tensions of the classroom/research dichotomy. (See Harriger and McMillan 2005.) When these tensions expanded to include our fellow citizens, however, the discomfort was palpable and challenged us and our students in unexpected ways.

Summary

Probably the Democracy Fellows will not look back on their community deliberation experience in Winston Salem as their finest hour. Certainly, it will not qualify as a "comfortable" encounter with the world outside the Wake Forest gates. Though they speak of their isolation from the community disparagingly, and repeatedly told us of desires to "leave their comfort zones," they were unprepared for the consequences of the short foray into community deliberation which they themselves had constructed and conducted. From our perspective as teachers and mentors of civic education, however, the experience—both its positive and negative aspects—may have been a fortuitous sample of true civic engagement.

Not only were students forced from their comfort zones, which many of them recognized was valuable, but their awareness of local problems with urban sprawl also increased dramatically. Creating the issue book required that they stretch their mental muscles in ways that expanded their critical thinking. Unpacking and contextualizing a complex national issue was especially challenging after the campus issue framing of familiar material. A secondary value of customizing the discussion of urban sprawl for their adopted city was the development of specific local dispositions.

The town/gown divide, which characterizes almost every college town, also plagues Winston-Salem, but Democracy Fellows truly believed that they had taken at least a small step toward fracturing the dividing wall by the hard work they had done on behalf of the community. Students spoke of the appreciation that they received for representing and addressing a pressing issue of local concern. Many students returned that appreciation with more civic empathy and social interaction.

On the other hand, they found their administrative and planning skills inadequate to the task; their networks small and ineffective; their publicity strategies woefully lacking; and their efforts at face-to-face recruiting uncomfortable and vulnerable. As opposed to the familiar territory of campus community, the problems of urban sprawl and the emotion the subject engendered seemed complex and daunting. And most critically, the students perceived that the community had stereotyped them as privileged college students who were doing "a little project" and were in over their heads. The second community deliberation at NCCEC offered some comfort, but the sting of the first remained.

Finally, in the midst of all the complexity that surrounded this deliberation effort, the last thing we or the students expected was to confront a moral dilemma as well. Should we as teachers and mentors move to rescue our students from possible failure, which might prevent their learning valuable lessons of civic engagement? Should we as researchers in pursuit of a "pure," objective study back off and watch dispassionately as the process floundered? Should we as community citizens intervene with expertise, which we clearly had, to help ensure the most productive outcome for the community we all share? These are not the questions we expected at the eleventh hour before the deliberation, but they are the ones we encountered.

CHAPTER SIX

The Senior Year Data

Chapter Six

The Senior Year Data

During the senior year, we were interested in discovering how the students' ideas about citizenship and politics had developed. Much of the work on political socialization focuses on the developmental nature of the process—that the notion of their roles as citizens unfolds over time as the result of experiences in family, school, and community (Colby et al. 2003; Gibson 2001; McLellan and Young 1997; Verba, Schlozman, and Brady 1995). Patrick (2000) recognizes the extent to which civic education is also about intellectual development, moving from learning the facts of political life to learning to live out democratic ideas as an active citizen. The Democracy Fellows project was designed with this developmental notion in mind. We began in the classroom during the first year and moved out into the practice and experience of deliberation in the second and third years. We decided not to plan any interventions with the group during their senior year. Instead, we would leave them to their own activities and schedules and interview them during the last semester of their senior year, along with a senior class cohort.[11]

---

[11] We conducted 25 individual interviews of about one hour each with the Democracy Fellows. In the four years, three students had transferred, one student was abroad that semester, and one failed to show up for the interview. We conducted three focus groups with a senior cohort drawn from students who had participated in our cohort focus groups in past years. (Some new students were added to the groups to ensure racial diversity.) We asked both groups the same questions we had asked them when they entered as first-year students, although this time, we asked them to look back at their experiences rather than to anticipate them. We added additional questions for the Democracy Fellows, assessing the deliberative model and the program. All interviews were audiotaped and transcribed. All interviewees filled out a participation survey of campus activities. Finally, we added questions to the annual HERI senior survey, which allowed us to compare attitudes of the Democracy Fellows and the senior cohort to the whole class.

In the interviews, we asked students in both groups to reflect on their four years of college experience, and, in the case of the Democracy Fellows, to reflect on the program itself. Their responses demonstrated to us two key findings.

First, as might be expected, it is clear that the experience of college itself, without any deliberative interventions, has a significant impact on the maturation of young people both intellectually and politically. A liberal education teaches students to think more critically and to pay some attention to the political world. As a group, the seniors left with more awareness about the political world—with questioning minds and, in many cases, with the inclination to critically analyze the world around them.

Second, we found that the experiences of the Democracy Fellows had a significant impact in giving them a more communal sense of citizenship, a set of democratic skills other students did not have, a greater democratic sensibility about what it meant to be a citizen in a democratic society, and a stronger sense of their own voice in campus governance. Interestingly, we also found that the Democracy Fellows were more critical of the American political system than their peers.

The Democracy Fellows

Politics. We began our interviews by asking students to think about the level of their interest in, and concerns about, politics. The Democracy Fellows talked about politics at many levels. For them, politics at the macro level meant "the workings of government," national campaigns, and what happens in Washington, D.C. At the micro level, politics was "people dealing with everyday issues." Some more thoughtful responses represented politics as process, power, and voice. One fellow descended the ladder of abstraction by starting in Washington, D.C., moving to local politics, and then identifying the political dimensions of all organizations. In short, definitions of politics for the fellows seemed to be broad and complex. While they clearly identified the more obvious political institutions, such as government and elections, they also mentioned as "political" things like community life, coexistence with others, and the everyday workings of their own campus organizations.

Not all Democracy Fellows expressed the enthusiasm of one student who remarked: "I love politics," but the vast majority affirmed that their interest in politics had been maintained over their four years at Wake Forest or had grown. Many expressed the savvy and caution of one young woman who said that after four years, she was "more knowledgeable but more confused." Only a small minority of fellows seemed to have lost their enthusiasm for politics, citing such disincentives as the outcome of the 2004 election and frustration with the U.S. political system. It was not uncommon for them to make a distinction between interest and optimism: "While my interest has continued, my optimism and sense of political efficacy has not."

Interestingly, the Democracy Fellows were considerably more negative about the *practice* of politics. They chose words like *jaded*, *cynical*, and *frustrated* to describe their feelings about how politics works, and they were particularly discouraged by the lack of participation by the public. One student called the 2000 election "illegitimate," and a number expressed dismay at the outcome of the 2004 election, (despite the fact that the group, at least when it entered college, reflected closely the ideological make-up of the overall class, whose members had expressed faith in the govern-mental system). The Democracy Fellows also characterized the system as slow, inefficient, polarized, and much too money-driven, when it comes to addressing significant issues, such as health care, poverty, and urban decay. Some of these same themes, especially the concerns about polarization and money in politics, had shown up in the first-year data. What was different in the senior year, however, was their recognition of the complexity of the system and their understanding that this complexity is tied to what they identi-fied as particular policy failures. Certainly, the sophistication of their analysis had increased.

On the other hand, the Democracy Fellows believed that by many countries' standards, the U.S. system has to be viewed as "operating well." More people did come out to vote in 2004, one student reminded us. And while many fellows saw political policy-making as lengthy and cumbersome, one student pointed out that extended discourse about an issue may avert hasty and thoughtless decision making. Though more than one fellow said that they had "lost faith in American politics," there was a spirit of optimism that generally pervaded the interviews, and several of them even used the word *hope* to describe their political outlook.

Despite the fact that the fellows found much to criticize in the current state of U.S. politics, they floundered in their efforts to identify specific changes that need to occur, either in political structure or practice. In contrast to their first-year answers, in which the most common solution they offered was amending the Electoral College, the most consistent theme in the senior year had to do with the communication of political information. Students were very critical, for example, of the media spin on political information. One fellow opined that his master correction would be "perfect information." Others mentioned various issues, such as proportional representation, redistricting, and even the criminal-justice system.

Democracy Fellows were clearer when asked what sorts of changes would be necessary to fit the students' images of how politics "should be." Here their enhanced understanding of the complexity of politics and their appreciation for its communicative aspects were clear. They pointed to flaws in the election process as failing to reflect the "voice of the people," and to help remedy that problem, they advocated improvement in campaign finance, the two-party system, and more referenda throughout the country. To help close the disconnect between themselves and their political leaders, the fellows admonished "the people" as well, urging more participation, more deliberation, and more dialogue. Most Democracy Fellows saw these changes as plausible, although one feared that it might take "a catastrophe" to jump-start active citizenship.

Citizenship. We wanted to know how students thought about citizenship generally and the extent to which they considered themselves to be active citizens. Several fellows were clear about distinguishing between the technical or legal citizenship that accrues from merely living in a country or locale, and the duties of citizenship that drive a flourishing democracy. Democracy Fellows identified voting as a baseline measure of responsibility, with political knowledge and understanding a very close second. Informing oneself of the issues—"paying attention"—was the key to civic responsibility and involved things like reading newspapers, watching newscasts, understanding political events and issues, and talking about them with friends and colleagues. As we see later in the participation survey data, Democracy Fellows were likely to get much of their information from reading newspapers rather than from television. This emphasis on knowledge and dialogue with others as keys to civic engagement was much stronger than it had been in the first-year interviews.

Many Democracy Fellows described altruism as an element of citizenship and used communal and value-laden language to explain the role of a "good" citizen. They talked about the importance of making "a better life for all" and argued that what we need in American politics is "less self-interest," "more dialogue," and "empowerment" of all citizens vis-à-vis politicians. This language was also in contrast to that which they had used in the first-year study when these students talked about good citizenship more in terms of voting and participation in political activity and less in terms of concern for others.

The university's role. Given our interest in the role of higher education in citizen education, we asked the students to assess the university's success in preparing them for citizenship. Almost unanimously these senior Democracy Fellows affirmed the role of the university as a civic training ground. One young woman who had recently been named a Rhodes scholar called college "a very strategic time" in the development of a budding citizen, and felt that colleges and universities should seize the opportunity to encourage responsible citizenship. Others agreed, but felt that colleges, even their own, generally prepared students more for a career than for an active life in a democracy. Another young man lamented: "I can't see a good education not doing that [training for citizenship]. I think, today, we focus too much on preparing a person for employment."

Several Democracy Fellows countered the notion that the responsibility was the institution's alone; they argued that the development of civic responsibility and awareness flows both ways. Colleges and universities should offer opportunities, they said, but students should seize and act on those opportunities. Some feared that the college years may even be too late, that civic activism should be engendered in the lower grades and only nurtured at the college level.

When asked to assess their own institution as a civic training ground, the fellows' opinions were mixed. Some felt that the institution was too concerned with its public face to spend adequate time and resources fostering citizenship. As one student put it: "It is a whole prestige thing. It is like Wake Forest wants the student to have the prestigious jobs so they can get more money." Others blamed their student peers for being "lazy" and "apathetic" where civic pursuits are concerned. Wake Forest provides opportunities in the form of public forums, such as the pre-election debate between the College Democrats and the College Republicans, an array of impressive speakers and events, and accessible professors who are willing to entertain both sides of an issue. Most consistently noted by students was that this veritable smorgasbord of political opportunities cannot be forced down the throats of unwilling students; students must respond and take advantage of these opportunities.

The Democracy Fellows' view on the question of the university's role seemed to have been tempered by their four years of experience. In their entrance interviews, they had had high expectations of what universities could and should do to promote civic engagement. By the time they were seniors they still viewed the school's role as important, but they saw the question as much more of a two-way street—universities should do more than they do, but so too should students.

Experiences that encouraged engagement. Looking back through their four years, we asked, what experiences stand out as encouraging civic involvement? Two strong factors encouraged these students to civic action: study abroad and their association with the Democracy Fellows program. As in previous years, students reported that time spent abroad was "eye-opening" and profound in terms of their political awareness and development. Jarred from their comfort zones and immersed in unfamiliar cultures, students turned a critical eye on both their host governments' political systems and practices and on those of their own country. Students talked about two primary reactions to the study-abroad experience. One was greater respect for the United States and the benefits of citizenship in their own country. The other was dismay, either with the American image abroad or at the contrast that they witnessed in participation among young people. They wondered aloud whether they or their peers would take to the streets as they saw some of their international counterparts doing. Many students mentioned their discovery that citizens of other countries were less impressed with U.S. democracy than they were. One fellow noted:

> Most everybody I talked to [thought] . . . the American government sort of put out this feeling, we don't care what you think, you know we are right, and we are . . . the world's superpower, and we are going to go in and fix everything, and our way is the best way, and if you can't do it our way, then, you have obviously failed, and we need to . . . educate you differently.

Many Democracy Fellows reported that study abroad catalyzed their impulse for civic engagement either through greater participation or the search for greater knowledge and understanding of their own country.

Participating in the Democracy Fellows program also served to encourage civic action. We will develop more fully the impact of deliberative training later, but reflecting on their college years, several students pointed to their first-year seminar in Deliberative Democracy and/or to the deliberations themselves—both on campus and in the community—as pivotal in advancing their personal impetus for political action. In particular, the success of the campus deliberation gave these students tangible evidence that civic progress is attainable, and they were especially buoyed by the practical outcomes (e.g., a new coffee house and a revised first-year orientation program), which seemed to have been outcomes of the deliberation.

While study abroad and the Democracy Fellows program dominated talk of civic catalysts, other campus influences were also mentioned. These included service-learning experiences, memorable classes led by professors who encouraged students to think about politics and issues, and various campus groups, such as the College Democrats and College Republicans, the Race Relations Committee, and Project Pumpkin, the on-campus social event at Halloween for underprivileged youngsters in the community. The primary external catalyst to political interest in 2004 was clearly the presidential election.

Finally, as further evidence that their conception of citizenship had developed into a more communal one, it is worth noting that a number of the Democracy Fellows felt that their education and experiences had helped lead to careers that involved service to others. For example, two male fellows joined Teach for America; another will work for a nonprofit; one young woman is committed to working with Hispanic children in the school system; another is pursuing a law degree in order to practice public interest law; and the Rhodes scholar is training for a public health medical career in her home country of Kenya, with a special interest in reducing infant mortality.

Experiences that discouraged engagement. While students spoke about those influences that had encouraged them, there were factors that mediated against their political enthusiasm as well. By far the strongest finding of effects that limit political activity was a continuation of the "citizenship deferred" theme we have documented throughout this study, although among the Democracy Fellows, this was not as strong as it was in their first-year responses. Two different students describe this phenomenon:

> When I get out of college and have more time, I definitely will participate a lot more. I think it is hard in college, when . . . you get so focused on . . . yourself, you know? . . . When I look at how I spend my days . . . I need to do this for school and this for school, and apply for this job, and, you know, at the end of the day it is just kind of . . . I don't know.

[I was] not necessarily as active as I should ideally be. It is just, kind of get my life in order for graduation. . . . I am more interested in my immediate life direction after graduation than I am in general politics.

Other negative influences for the Democracy Fellows broke along macro and micro issues. At the macro level, the elections of 2000 and 2004 discouraged many; some identified the outcome of the 2004 election as leaving them in "limbo" and sapped of political energy. One male Democracy Fellow even admitted that for a time following the election, he "wanted to leave the U.S." Other students mentioned the Electoral College, political corruption, and negative campaigns. Micro factors of discouragement had to do with a campus political culture that students regarded as "conservative," "apathetic," "intolerant," "self-interested," and clearly isolated from the community surrounding it. Even a recent student referendum concerning the choice of a new meal plan did not convince many of the fellows that students truly have political power and influence.

Reassessing the Four Models of Civic Engagement

As we did four years earlier, we asked the Democracy Fellows to consider four different models for how universities might prepare them for citizenship and to assess the likely effectiveness of each model. While they had newfound appreciation for the importance of knowledge gained in the classroom, they continued their enthusiasm for the service learning model. Most important, after four years of experience with the deliberative skills model, they were able to talk critically and in depth about its strengths and drawbacks as an approach to civic education.

The traditional academic model. A significant number of Democracy Fellows believed that there is value in learning about politics and the potential for civic action in the classroom, especially studying the "classic texts." While some students found traditional methods "boring" and "impractical," they virtually all agreed that such material is "foundational" to political enlightenment and that if students have not been adequately prepared in high school, colleges and universities should assume the responsibility. There was much more appreciation expressed for this model than there had been in the first-year data, and student responses here were quite consistent with the newly found value that knowledge and understanding are important prerequisites to good citizenship. One fellow believed that the political science courses he had taken "worked for me ... I understand the political process better." Students were quick to point out, however, that an autocratic classroom where teachers lecture without discussion and peers debate without reflection can quickly turn the traditional classroom into an endurance contest.

Service learning. As was true with the first-year data, service learning was a method of student engagement highly favored by virtually all Democracy Fellows. They liked the hands-on aspect of this model, which forces them to face the real problems of real people whom they have only read about in the traditional classroom. One fellow called service learning "inspiring"; another said that it forces students to witness the "face of the problem," and yet another opined that service learning "holds promise."

Despite their enthusiasm for this option, the fellows were careful to qualify their endorsement. They believed that service-learning programs are often poorly conducted and that students fail to respect them, dutifully logging their hours without enthusiasm or without much engagement with the social or political issues involved with the experience. In fact, several fellows were skeptical that students make the connection between the service exercise and its political root or implication. However, when the connection is made, students see service learning as an excellent venue for political activism. Two students offered eloquent testimonies of service experiences in Winston-Salem, one with the local activist group CHANGE, and the other with an internship whose goal was to bring the DELL computer company to the region. The latter reported:

> I was amazed to watch this summer the people who stepped up to help bring DELL to town. Like these leaders who,

you can't see that they would necessarily have this huge gain because they're already pretty well off and you're talking about some of them even bringing a competitor to town, but they recognize it is what is best for this town and what is best for the people . . . so they're willing to chip in, whether it's monetarily or time or going to politic with the governor.

Democratizing the campus. This option of making campuses more democratic communities continued to generate a wide variety of reaction. Many Democracy Fellows were highly enthusiastic about the potential of more student involvement in campus governance. One exuded: "I wish. I do. I do." Students pointed to the recent campus vote on the meal-plan options as an example of how such democratization *could* work. Many alluded to a sense of powerlessness that could be abated by a more democratic campus climate. Not surprisingly, they identified the seat of power where such a change must be implemented as "the administration."

As noted previously, however, some asserted that the administration was not the sole culprit—that indeed students often fail to take advantage of the opportunities of governance that they are afforded. Democracy Fellows were hard on themselves and student peers, suggesting that additional democracy might not work because students can be "unreliable," "self-interested," "unable to see the big picture," and "lack the maturity" to govern effectively. Democracy Fellows did believe, however, that democratizing the campus was a "good option" if the administration would risk relinquishing power and if students proved up to the task. They were hopeful, that with more student voice, cynicism would dramatically decrease. The impact of their experience with the campus deliberation seemed apparent here. While in the first year they had expressed an equal amount of skepticism of this model and lack of understanding of how it might work, in the senior year their comments revealed much more appreciation for its potential.

Teaching deliberative skills. After four years of exposure to the deliberative model of public talk, Democracy Fellows generally were quite favorably disposed toward the idea, characterizing it in such terms as: *a good model, hopeful, a wonderful program, teaches good political education.* Because assessing the effectiveness of this model is central to this research project, we asked students 1) to compare the model to the other pedagogical forms we had proposed; 2) to list the advantages and disadvantages of deliberation which they had seen and/or experienced; and 3) to identify any aspect of the deliberative model that they might be using in their lives, and if so, where and how it had been useful. We evaluated their responses by considering whether they were identifying knowledge acquisition, cognitive development, participatory skills, or dispositions of citizenship (Patrick 2000) as the forms of learning they had experienced.

While the responses of the Democracy Fellows demonstrated some elements of all four of Patrick's components of civic education, it was clear that the two strongest effects of the program identified by these students were the creation of *democratic dispositions* and the development of *participatory skills*, although *political knowledge* and *cognitive development* were clearly reflected in their answers as well.

As one Democracy Fellow contended, and others agreed in one way or another, deliberation has the potential to "revitalize American politics." Reflecting the development of *dispositions of citizenship* and democratic sensibilities, they believed that participating in deliberations had increased their political engagement and would have a similar effect on others if they were given a similar opportunity. They identified as deliberation's positive impacts on them, the willingness to keep an open mind when listening to others, the ability to take another person's perspective and articulate it fairly, the ability to consider alternatives and examine the trade-offs in different choices, and the recognition that decision making should involve many voices and fair processes for those voices to be heard. Many fellows appreciated what they saw as the citizen-equity issues that deliberation addressed. They talked about how it "leveled the playing field" and "appealed to both the cynical and the voiceless."

The Democracy Fellows also identified *participatory skills* that they believed had been fostered by their deliberative experiences. These included an improved ability to listen to others, to articulate their own views in public settings, and to act as moderators in discussions in their organizations, workplaces, friendships, and families. One student noted that the skills had broad application beyond the political realm; "You can do it anywhere," noted one enthusiast. The students also believed that their experiences had had positive practical implications for their class work, both in participating in class discussion and in researching and writing. One Democracy Fellow summed it up, saying that deliberation is "an overall skill that students need," not just to be citizens but to be more effective in their daily lives.

Their *acquisition of knowledge* and *cognitive development*, especially with regard to critical thinking, were evident as well. Consistent with the critical spirit of these Democracy Fellows, they also were clear about the limitations that they perceived in the deliberation model and they did not hesitate to tell us about them. While their general assessment of the model was positive, they used words like *systematic* (acknowledging that deliberation must be taught and practiced), *intimidating*, *demanding*, and *formal* to describe aspects of the model they found difficult. More specific, they described deliberation as challenging to learn and to practice. Here they referenced their continuing memories of the difficult race-relations deliberation in the first-year seminar and the community deliberation they had organized in their junior year. They noted the difficulty of soliciting participation by a diverse group of citizens and the level of commitment required by the organizers and participants. They also had some concerns about the slowness of the process, especially if it is used in larger community settings to try to bring about change. As we have found throughout the study, they had concerns about getting to action through deliberation. Many of the Democracy Fellows remain skeptical about this stage of the model. Talking is valuable, they believe, but in the end, if politics is to change, action must be taken.

The Senior Cohort

The comparison group was asked the same set of questions as the Democracy Fellows, although we probed much more deeply with the fellows about the deliberative model.

Politics. The responses of the group to questions about what politics meant to them fell roughly into three categories, from stronger to weaker trends: institutional, attitudinal, and procedural. At the institutional level, most seniors mentioned elements of "formal" government: offices, elections, voting, the Electoral College. They also were quick to reveal attitudes about politics that tended to be negative, using descriptors like *frustrating*, *overwhelming*, *flawed*, *impotent*, and *divided*. One student said, "I wouldn't say that I am indifferent, but . . . I'm frustrated about it." Another said, "Every time I think about it, I think it is just too overwhelming to even start digging into." Finally, a few focused on the process of politics by mentioning things like lobbying, discussion, negotiation, and debate. Here, they tended to return to the negative descriptors, pointing out the protracted nature of political discussion and how difficult policy is to decide upon and to implement. One student, who said that he believed he had learned a lot more about politics while in college, said that nonetheless, he was still "kind of disinterested just because I don't see anything happening." In contrast to the first-year data, many students thought they had more knowledge about the system in their senior year, but that knowledge had not translated into any greater sense of empowerment or interest.

When asked about how well they thought the system was working and what they would change about it, they revealed the roots of their generally negative descriptions about politics. While most thought the system worked "fairly well," they tended to emphasize this in a comparative sense, noting that many other systems did not work well at all. Their institutional focus carried over to their assessment of the system—they tended to think that the structural/constitutional framework of the system worked and generally would not change anything about it, with the exception of the Electoral College. Their criticisms of the system tended to focus instead on the processes of national politics—how candidates get selected, the role of money and interest groups in the system, and the polarization of the political parties. A few students made distinctions between groups of people in terms of how well the system worked, arguing that it worked well for the educated and wealthy but "not at all in the Mississippi Delta," where one of them had spent a summer during college. He said, "It [the Constitution and the Bill of Rights] should have worked out, but liberty and justice for all didn't happen." For the most part, these students' attitudes about politics had not changed much since their first year. They tended to focus on the same issues at the same level of analysis, despite claiming to know more about the system. They did seem to be slightly more critical of American politics than they had been as first-year students, whose patriotic expressions at the time were no doubt heightened by the then-recent terrorist attacks of September 11, 2001.

Citizenship. As with the Democracy Fellows, a strong theme throughout the senior cohort's responses to questions about citizenship focused on knowledge and understanding of politics and policy as important civic indicators. They considered themselves to be active citizens if they were spending time reading or watching the news and trying to keep up with current events. They tended to see knowledge as critical to the ability to act. Interestingly, they also saw discussion of issues as part of being active and, as several suggested, "politics is talk." They mentioned quite frequently their participation with other students in discussions as examples of their political engagement.

Students also tended to distinguish between legalistic notions of citizenship (e.g., voting, residency) and "active" or "good" citizenship, which requires actual political engagement beyond voting. In contrast to the Democracy Fellows, among the senior cohort there was a noticeable tendency to define citizenship in quite individualistic terms, focusing on participation to protect one's self-interest, and getting involved because of the realization that "next year we are going to be in the real world and we are going to be affected by taxes, and whatnot." Students often tied their newfound knowledge of the system with this self-interest. One student, talking about how his interest in politics had increased during his time in college, noted that he had "learned how to make the government . . . work for me . . . how it can actually be manipulated in a sense, to help me get what I want." Another said that "if you need something changed, it is more of a question of knowing the rules and how the system works." Still another said he thought of the system as both something that "caters to you as an individual" and something "like an interest in sports, or a hobby, or something like that."

There were a few students in this group who expressed a broader or more communal sense of their citizenship. "Whether it is inter-acting with people in the community, getting to know them and their views of what they would like, and trying to understand people better," one young woman said, citizenship is about "getting out and not hiding in your house away from people but knowing people around you in situations, and being knowledgeable." Another student said her definition of citizenship was "being compassionate with your neighbors and other people in the United States and globally."

Students who considered themselves inactive citizens had a range of explanations for this inactivity, but they tended to focus on the now-familiar notion of citizenship deferred. The inclination to "put off" civic participation continued to be a robust finding among students in the cohort, suggesting little change from the early data.

The university's role. There was almost universal agreement among the senior cohort that universities have a role to play in preparing students for their roles as citizens, but most seemed to think that the key role is to provide opportunity, without coercion, to become engaged. Again, in the individualistic language identified above, they argued that it should be up to the student to decide whether to take advantage of the opportunities offered them; some will, some won't, and that's okay with these respondents. As one student commented, "I don't think a university can *make* you be interested in anything. . . . If you are interested in politics you will do that." Another said, "I think the university is just supposed to provide access. . . . No one should force their personal, particular beliefs or moral beliefs or whatever it is on you." This is in contrast to the Democracy Fellows, who also talked about the university providing opportunities, but framed the students' role as one of responsibility to take up those opportunities, not just as an individual choice.

Most of the students in the comparison group seemed to think that Wake Forest was doing fairly well in this regard, providing many opportunities to be involved with student government, clubs and organizations, and community service and bringing in speakers who represented different points of view about issues. Many students mentioned the recent campus visit by James Carville, former aide to President Bill Clinton and liberal news commentator, as a positive example of the university providing an opportunity to learn.

Experiences that encouraged engagement. Senior cohort students spoke appreciatively of classroom opportunities for discussion of political and social issues and of professors who did not "force" their own views on the students. They liked professors who "encourage you to think for yourself" and who are willing to "play the devil's advocate." They also thought that hearing the different views of their peers in classroom and informal discussions was motivating, either because it made them realize that they needed to know more, or their disagreement with the views expressed made them want to participate to counteract those views. One student noted that, in contrast to high school, during college he had been "surrounded by people who are active in politics." He attributed his own interest in activism to this peer influence. Another also noted the influence of friends: "I have friends . . . I disagree with politically. We still manage to have good, healthy conversations about it, and I think that has a lot to do with [his interest]." One young man talked about two friends who "happen to be on two different ends" of the political spectrum and how "neat" it was "to listen to two people debate it, and for me to hear, because that has helped me to form some opinion."

Students who had studied abroad almost universally described this as a positive experience, which had expanded their notions of citizenship (several talked about "global citizenship") and had motivated them to be more involved in their own system. One student expressed her surprise in discovering on a service trip to Vietnam that "everything worked so well." It also gave her an appreciation of her own country and the rights protected here. In discussing her conversations with Vietnamese students about their government, she learned that they did not feel free to speak out against their government the way American students did. Another student who spent the summer in a "lesser developed country" said, "It really made me take an interest in what is going on in the world and how things in the world are so different than we are, and why, and which way is better." Even students who had not been abroad themselves could be influenced by people who had. One young woman talked about her roommate who had returned after a year in Spain and Chile with a rather critical view of the United States and its foreign policy. "Her interest in that is kind of fueling my interest," she said. "I'm kind of mad at myself for being so dumb about politics, because she talks about it all the time, and I am like, I don't know what you are saying."

Experiences that discouraged engagement. Just as they appreciated professors who stayed neutral and encouraged all points of view, the seniors disliked professors who pushed one point of view, particularly if it was one with which they disagreed. (One student somewhat sheepishly admitted that the perceived conservative bias in his business classes bothered him less than the perceived liberal bias in his politics courses.) Students talked about professorial bias as being "unfair" and sometimes "intimidating," especially for first- and second-year students.

Specialization in majors other than the social sciences also tends to turn people away from political engagement. Several students noted the lack of opportunity for discussion of anything, much less politics, in courses in the science and math areas. In addition to content, students talked in general about the heavy workload and how the academic pressures mediate against civic engagement.

This theme has been present throughout the four years of our study and, while still strong in the class cohort, actually seemed less dominant this year than in previous years. The presidential election of 2004 seemed to have captured the attention of even the most committed science majors! And, inevitably, there was a set of concerns particular to seniors: Who has time for politics when we are "worrying about what we are doing next year," trying to get a job, or applying to graduate school?

Students frequently pointed to the campus climate as discouraging engagement. In particular, they raised the problem of being removed from the community and out of touch with what goes on off-campus. They attributed this to the location of the university (a gated campus on the edge of the city) and to the kind of students who attend the university (highly academically motivated, affluent, and uninterested in those unlike themselves). They also thought the lack of student power on campus and the way in which power was exercised by the administration was discouraging. They talked about a disputed student government election and a controversial decision to change the food service as examples that turned them off to campus involvement. Few, however, seemed to have done much to burst the Wake Forest bubble or challenge policy changes, reflecting a continuing theme of complaint combined with little sense of efficacy about how problems might be overcome.

Reassessing the Four Models of Civic Engagement in Higher Education

We also asked the senior cohort to consider four different models for how universities might prepare them for citizenship and to assess their likely effectiveness. As they did in their first year, members of the comparison group tended to see the ideal as being some combination of the traditional academic, the service learning, the democratic campus, and the deliberative skills models. Perhaps not surprisingly, given their four years of classroom experience and the emphasis they put on knowledge acquisition in being an effective citizen, they too had more appreciation for the traditional academic model in the fourth year than they had had in their first year.

The traditional academic model. One student seemed to capture the most common sentiment of the group concerning the traditional classroom model by saying it was "necessary but not motivational." Others emphasized the "foundational" nature of knowledge to citizenship and the classroom as an important place to acquire that knowledge. Students who had had political science or other social-science classes seemed to have greater appreciation for the role that the classroom could play than those who had followed tracks that focused on the acquisition of scientific knowledge. There continued to be the assumption in the discussion of this model that its general success would depend on whether one was a political science major—in other words, generally seeing this kind of knowledge as specialized and necessary for those who had an affinity for or interest in it, rather than as central for all citizens.

Some students were able to imagine the classroom as a place for much more than simply the transfer of specific factual knowledge. One young man eloquently recommended the give-and-take of a dynamic classroom when he said:

> I think my biggest motivator here is sitting in the classroom having the teacher ask the question to the class and hearing another student respond and I'm thinking how come I don't know about that or how come I've never thought of that?

So while many students responded as if they were describing the passive transfer of knowledge about political texts or even a monologue from a professor, this student captured the interactive possibility of discussion in his assessment of the model. Some students also mentioned courses that involved a service component as being valuable classroom experiences, which challenged the "traditional" boundaries of the classroom.

Service learning. Most of the class cohort expressed enthusiasm for the idea that experiential learning and exposure to things you cannot see in the classroom can have a significant impact on student engagement. They saw this as a particularly important way to break out of the bubble of their campus life. They did make distinctions between service *requirements* that were not monitored or clearly integrated into the course, and service *learning* where the connections between the service and the class were more clearly made. As we had already found, the control-group students were very much against the notion of "forcing" service because they perceived insincere service as being unlikely to change anyone's mind or heart. They were somewhat skeptical that the experience of "seeing a problem" would necessarily lead to the inclination to do something about it, but some thought such a connection was possible. Several expressed rather cynical views that most people do service as "résumé building" rather than out of sincere motivation to address community problems, and one said about her experience with mandatory service, "I hated every minute of it." One more optimistic senior, however, suggested that if even one student out of a group "gets it," then it has been a worthwhile effort. She also thought there ought to be more focus on practical outcomes rather than on how people felt about the experience. If people tutor young children, for example, and some of those kids end up being able to read, then that outcome is more important than whether the students doing the tutoring liked it or not, she argued.

Democratizing the campus. Seniors tended to respond to the idea of democratizing the campus in the same way they had in their first year. They seemed conflicted by this choice, to the extent that they understood it. Many of them had trouble imagining what it would mean to have a democratic campus and the interviewers had to explain it in more detail. While it was very appealing to some (and they pointed to successful examples of democratized dorm living at MIT and Rice University, where friends attended school), many others were skeptical that it would work on campus. They cited the outgoing administration as undemocratic and "disconnected," and they felt that students did not have an adequate voice in the recent presidential search. Upon reflection, they admitted that participation had been offered in forums and speak-outs, but that few students had availed themselves of the opportunities. This realization led them to the more serious and pervasive critique of this option-—that students were not mature or committed enough to be included in campus governance. The senior cohort used these words to describe themselves and their peers: *apathetic, lazy, lacking political knowledge, too busy,* and lacking the *big picture.* To the dismay of some of the others, one student even called democratizing the campus "dangerous." By far the quintessential quote on this option was from one female student who said: "You can't give us too much power because we are a group of people who can go out to bars now … to drink, but we still watch cartoons!"

Beyond the question of whether students were capable of actively participating in campus governance, there was skepticism about whether a truly democratized campus would actually be an effective way to encourage civic engagement among young people. Some students who were skeptical about the broader political system thought that teaching students democratic skills this way would actually prepare them for disillusionment when they found out that "the real world doesn't work that way."

Teaching deliberative skills. At least in the abstract, the senior cohort found some appeal in this model, but their general skepticism about people's motivation to participate in politics carried over here as well. There was quite a bit of enthusiasm throughout the focus group interviews for opportunities to talk, discuss, and debate issues, and they identified these experiences as important motivators for themselves in getting involved. Yet when presented with a model that would seek to provide more opportunities for this on campus, they defaulted to their standard concerns about something like this "taking too much time," not producing "action," and not being appealing to students. The concerns about whether this model would actually prepare students for the real world of politics, (one that they see as about self-interest, power, and money) were raised here as well. One rather lukewarm response—"It wouldn't hurt"—seemed to reflect the views of many. Interestingly, some recognized that the focus groups that they have participated in for this project might be similar to what this model entails, and they admitted to enjoying the focus group discussions. Their answers on the senior survey, which we will discuss later, suggest that participation just in these annual events may have had some impact on their evaluation of their campus experience with regard to civic engagement.

Comparing the Two Groups

The interviews revealed some commonalities between the two groups, as well as a number of differences.

Commonalities. Both the Democracy Fellows and students in the senior cohort assessed the current political climate similarly. Nationally, they believe that money and power play too great a role in the political process and yearn for the time when the "voice of the people" will be restored and "ordinary folks" can run for political office. Both groups consider themselves to be fairly "active" politically, having voted in the presidential election, although there were a number of students in the senior cohort who remained largely uninterested and uninvolved. On campus, both groups agree that students have about as much power as they are willing to assume, that indeed authority figures, especially in the administration, may overfunction politically because students lack the maturity and commitment to share more of the role of campus governance. There are, however, some differences in their sense of efficacy when it comes to responding to this power imbalance.

A final surprising commonality among both groups was the importance of "talk" as political action. Neither group identified this as important to civic engagement during their first year. But by the senior year, both groups lauded the classes in which they were allowed to express their opinions, and valued the opportunities to discuss issues with their peers, even when opinions and views may differ. While we might have expected this inflation of political expression among the Democracy Fellows for whom it had been a central part of their training, the same yearning for, and valuing of, oral expression was strong across the board, highly recommending deliberation's most basic feature as a promising avenue to civic engagement.

Differences. Despite the many ways these two groups of senior students are alike, if one applies Patrick's benchmark of successful civic pedagogy, it appears that the Democracy Fellows outperform their senior peers in virtually every category—something that was not true when we began the study. Despite the fact that they majored in many different areas, Democracy Fellows seemed to have more knowledge and understanding of the intricacies of the democratic process and its challenges than did the senior cohort. The fellows talked about politics as a complex and multilayered process with opportunities for impact and influence locally and within one's organizations. Comparison-group seniors were fixated on a notion of politics that was simplistic, nationally focused, and conflictual —perhaps reflecting the fact that most of their information comes from television. Clearly, the political science majors in both groups displayed the most sophisticated assessment of the political system and its operations, which their training would predict. However, even Democracy Fellows who had chosen majors in business, communication, biology, psychology, and economics displayed the cognitive skills that Patrick alludes to as they described, analyzed, explained, and evaluated issues and the current political scene.

Democracy Fellows also appeared to excel in the understanding and the use of the deliberative model itself, or the "participative" elements of civic education Patrick describes. As would be expected, the distance between the fellows and their class cohort appeared most prominently in their respective descriptions of deliberation. While the seniors in the comparison group tended to default to some description of a "Crossfire" debate which they had often viewed on television, Democracy Fellows identified the subtleties which set apart deliberation from such adversarial formats; they mentioned active listening, identifying common values, and learning how to entertain the position of the "other." It was also striking how mindful the fellows were of the deliberative strategies they had learned and were using widely, in everything from help-ing friends solve problems, leading their campus organizations, improving their classroom participation, and interviewing well for jobs. In short, Democracy Fellows were capable of analyzing critically, and using, the successful strategies of public discussion which the class cohort largely took for granted or about which they were mostly unaware.

Finally, the difference in "dispositions of citizenship" between the two groups was striking, and their language told the story. By far the largest catalyst of political interest and action for the senior cohort was self-interest (e.g., health care, Social Security, the economy). One student put it plainly: "Politics must affect me directly to gain my interest." Another said: "I'm interested but not involved." And yet another senior said: "I see politics as somebody else's problem."

The Democracy Fellows, on the other hand, used more communal language and justified their interest in politics and their participation on the basis of making "a better life for all." In rather stark contrast to the descriptions of the senior cohort, when asked what it would take to align politics with their preferred vision, a number of Democracy Fellows mentioned "*less* self-interest." Others spoke of "participation," "empowerment," "less disconnect between the politicians and the people," and "more dialogue."

This contrasting view of the two groups is not meant to suggest that there were no outliers in all directions and within both groups. It does suggest, however, that somewhere in the course of their four-year matriculation at Wake Forest, the Democracy Fellows had developed decidedly more robust democratic dispositions, which Patrick argues are characterized by the promotion of the general welfare, recognition of the common humanity of each person, respecting and protecting rights, taking responsibility for one's participation, and supporting democratic principles and practices.

Survey Data

In addition to the interviews, we administered surveys to both groups to probe their perception of activism and voice on campus and their level of engagement in political and social activities. The responses indicated that both groups have strong levels of engagement in community service at Wake Forest. With percentages consistently above 80 percent for all survey years, most students are seeking community involvement as their activity of choice. Such consistent levels of involvement for both groups suggest that there may be a general feeling of obligation for students at

Wake Forest to engage in community service. Still, there was a slight tendency for the class cohort to be more involved than Democracy Fellows, suggesting that the typical student may engage in community service as a substitute for political activism. Students in the comparison group were also more likely to be spending their time in social activities, particularly in Greek organizations.

In contrast, Democracy Fellows were more likely to be involved in political activism than seniors in the comparison group. The high level of participation in political activities among Democracy Fellows indicates that they may be more politically "in tune" than the average student, due to their participation in the program. Democracy Fellows were more likely to have voted in the last election, participated in a political campaign, joined a political group that addressed social issues, written a letter to the editor of the newspaper, and read a newspaper. Students in the class cohort were more likely to say they were not at all active in politics and to identify television as their main source of political information.

It is also the case that Democracy Fellows consistently appeared less positive about the political system than their class cohort. (While few students from either category were willing to say that the U.S. political system is failing, there was a significant difference between the Democracy Fellows and the class cohort in giving the U.S. political system an extremely positive rating.) These percentages suggest that Democracy Fellows may have thought more critically about these issues than other students as a result of their political education.

The senior survey data gathered annually by HERI and our Office of Institutional Research provides another interesting contrast between the Democracy Fellows and their classmates. (See Table 3.) In this data, we were able to compare the fellows with the smaller class cohort and with the overall class. As the interview and participation survey data revealed, the community-service orientation remains strong in all three groups and most students leave Wake Forest feeling that they have been well prepared to serve their community.

Table 3
Campus Experience: Comparison
of Three Subject Groups

Community Service[a]			
	All WFU Seniors	Senior Cohort	Democracy Fellows
Great Deal	33%	21%	35%
Somewhat	43%	43%	29%
Unsure	13%	14%	24%
Very Little	8%	7%	12%
Not at All	3%	14%	0%

Campus Governance[b]			
	All WFU Seniors	Senior Cohort	Democracy Fellows
Great Deal	4%	7%	18%
Somewhat	21%	29%	41%
Unsure	16%	21%	12%
Very Little	43%	43%	18%
Not at All	16%	0%	12%

Civic Education[c]			
	All WFU Seniors	Senior Cohort	Democracy Fellows
Great Deal	16%	29%	29%
Somewhat	41%	36%	41%
Unsure	16%	21%	18%
Very Little	20%	7%	12%
Not at All	8%	7%	0%

*Results are rounded.

Note: The complete survey questions read as follows: [a] To what degree has your college education prepared you to serve your community? [b] To what degree did you think you had a voice in campus governance while at Wake Forest? [c] To what degree has your education prepared you to be active politically?

The strongest difference between the Democracy Fellows and other students had to do with their sense of having had a voice in campus governance. Combining the numbers in the top two positive response categories ("great deal" and "somewhat"), one sees that 59 percent of the fellows believed they had had a voice, while only 36 percent of those in the senior cohort, and a mere 25 percent of those in the whole senior class felt similarly. On the lower end of the scale, among those who felt they had had little or no voice in campus governance, the pattern reverses, with only 30 percent of fellows feeling this way, 43 percent of the cohort feeling this way, and a surprising 59 percent of the whole class feeling that they had little or no voice.

The Democracy Fellows were also the most likely to feel that the university had prepared them for active citizenship (70 percent in the top two response categories), with the class cohort being next with 65 percent and the entire class coming in last at 57 percent. On the negative end of the scale, only 12 percent of the Democracy Fellows and 14 percent of the class cohort felt that the university had not prepared them for active citizenship, while 28 percent of the whole class felt this way.

Particularly in the area of preparation for active citizenship, but also to some extent in the question of campus voice, we see that the class cohort diverged from the entire class and shared some commonalities with the Democracy Fellows. This may be explained, in part, by the fact that the cohort, with its small numbers was probably not representative of the class, but we suspect it may also be the influence of having participated for four years in our study, in which they were asked regularly to discuss and reflect on citizenship and political engagement. As we noted earlier, the senior cohort spoke enthusiastically about the opportunity the focus groups had afforded them to have interesting discussions. In general, the quantitative data seems to reinforce the findings from the qualitative data—participation in the Democracy Fellows program had a positive impact on students' sense of efficacy and confidence in being active citizens. But it may suggest an unexpected finding as well—that participation in regular discussions about politics in a less-structured, more sporadic program may also have positive benefits for students.

Summary

There will be more to say in the final chapter about what these findings mean for institutions of higher education. What is worth pointing out here is that, clearly, as one of our Democracy Fellows noted, the college years are a "strategic time" for nurturing citizen engagement. Our findings suggest that this is a time when young people's emerging citizenship is quite fragile—it can be both encouraged and discouraged. There is much competing for their attention and engagement, and they can be easily discouraged by what they experience and observe around them. Providing students with an alternative view of what politics might be and how citizenship might be exercised may have the ironic effect of causing students to cast a critical eye upon their political system and their own education. Challenges to the institution might come in two forms—discouragement and cynicism when the ideal does not fit the reality, or, student activism which could increasingly demand a voice at the table—the latter a more troubling outcome, no doubt, for those administrators who give lip service to engagement but prefer the status quo of power distribution on the campus.

CHAPTER SEVEN

Overall Findings

Chapter Seven

Overall Findings

To understand and to explicate higher education's role in civic education, we have pursued answers around three basic questions: Did students who learned to deliberate about public issues develop different democratic sensibilities than their peers who did not? What might be the effect of context—classroom, campus, and community—on the deliberative experience? How did the college experience generally shape students' attitudes and behavior about civic engagement? In this chapter, we compile and summarize our overall findings around those three issues. As we do so, the reader will notice that there is both confirmatory evidence of past literature and research and wholly new "wrinkles" that this unique longitudinal vantage point made visible. We believe both perspectives are important.

The Impact of Deliberation

Despite the commonalities of the students when they entered college, those who learned and practiced deliberation for four years were qualitatively different from their classmates who did not.

Democracy fellows were more involved in the traditional venues of political action that predict political involvement. Results of our study paralleled national trends in the popularity and frequency of community service among college students (Clymer 2000; Eyler and Giles 1999; Jacoby 1996); in fact, many, especially in the cohort, agreed with their counterparts from the Wingspread conference,[12] who see service as an "alternative politics" (Campus Compact 2002, 2). This attraction to service was true of virtually all the

---

[12] On March 15-17, 2001, 33 juniors and seniors representing 27 colleges and universities across the country met at the Johnson Foundation in Racine, Wisconsin, to consider together their civic experiences in higher education. Their three-day deliberations yielded a formal document of assessment and recommendations entitled *Campus Compact*.

students we interviewed. However, as we reported in Chapter Six, as the study progressed the Democracy Fellows separated themselves from the class cohort in two ways: They were 1) slightly less inclined toward community service than the class cohort, and 2) consistently more involved in traditional avenues of politics, such as voting, helping in a political campaign, joining a political group that focuses on a social issue, writing letters to the editor, and reading a newspaper. These findings are important because they suggest that the typical Wake Forest student could be substituting service for civic action, which many have feared (see, for example, Cooper 2004; Morse 1993; Neary 2003), while Democracy Fellows developed a wider, more expansive political repertoire which may eventually translate beyond college to political activism (McLellan and Youniss 1997; Verba, Schlozman and Brady 1995). There was a clear difference between the class cohort, who seemed to prefer service to politics, and the Democracy Fellows, who seemed less inclined toward service. One member of the student cohort captured the difference well: "[In politics] you never see a change . . . standing up on your soap box . . . and [politics] takes so many people . . . but it just takes one person to go teach a kid how to read or to, like, feed someone. I would rather do that." It is troubling that the same individual might fail to recognize that "standing on one's soap box" may be directly relevant to the fact that the kid can't read or that people are hungry.

Democracy Fellows were more attuned to the responsibilities of active citizenship. Prior to September 11, 2001, the data concerning a sense of civic responsibility among young people were grim (Bennett and Bennett 2001; Delli Carpini 2000), with many young people lamenting that either they did not have enough information to make a good decision and/or they did not think their vote could make a difference (Center for Information and Research on Civic Learning and Engagement 2002). Clearly, the picture has changed some since the terror attacks provided what *Newsweek* calls the "defining moment" for a generation that "once had it all—peace, prosperity, and even the dot-com dream of retiring at 30" (Kantrowitz et al. 2001, 46). While all students in our study struggled with current definitions of citizenship and what it requires of them, the differences between the Democracy Fellows and students in the cohort came down to small distinctions between political passivity and political activity.

While there were some exceptions, the cohort students spoke in more cavalier terms about civic responsibility and more frequently buffered themselves from political action. The events of 9/11 notwithstanding, the student who opined that "politics is somebody else's business" captured a predominant sentiment of the cohort. These students saw their civic responsibility mainly as "keeping up" (i.e., having adequate political knowledge, understanding policy, reviewing current events), which the participation surveys demonstrated that they did primarily through the medium of television. Those surveys also reinforced their passivity where more overt civic activities were concerned.

What stands out, however, when one peruses the citizenship talk of the Democracy Fellows is their frequent use of the words *action* or *engagement*. Though they too struggled with the differences between what they often called "technical" versus "good" citizenship, it is clear that for them, *citizenship* came to mean "doing something" about politics. Besides the data from the participation surveys that reinforced the fellows' political activity, they transferred their action imperative to the success of deliberation as well: "I must do more than appreciate this model, I must *promote* it and *commit myself* to action on the decisions made in deliberations" (emphasis added). "One of the best ways I can demonstrate the effectiveness of deliberation is to *invite* members of my community to participate." (Emphasis added.) "I know I can *make a difference* when I graduate from Wake. . . . I can *take my knowledge* of deliberation to the placeI work, I can also *teach* my children. . . . I will *participate* in social discussions more and I will *encourage* everyone I know to do soas well." (Emphasis added.)

Democracy Fellows were more analytical and critical of political processes and their role in them. Many (Gastil 2000; Gastil and Dillard 1999a; Gastil and Dillard 1999b; Osborn and Osborn 1991) have argued that not only is it important that young people learn to think about politics, but the way they think about politics may be equally important (Prince 2000). Recall that Patrick (2000) specifies the cognitive skills of civic engagement as identification, description, analysis, explanation, evaluation, and critical thinking. In Patrick's descriptors, one notices the communication activities of both encoding (initiating political messages by framing, shaping, refining, and delivering them *to* others) and decoding (identifying, assessing, evaluating political messages *from* others) (Beebe and Masterson 2000; Lucas 2004). Rhetorical scholars as far back as Aristotle, Cicero, and Quintillian recognized this mental agility as a gift of nature, but also one that could be developed and fine-tuned by training, such as what the Democracy Fellows experienced in their first semester and practiced throughout their four years at Wake Forest.

Shortly after the first-year seminar experience, we began to notice what we came to call "sophistication" in the way these students thought and talked about politics. (See Gastil and Dillard's (1999b) perspective on political sophistication as the coherent integration and differentiation of beliefs; see also McLeod, et al. for a parallel discussion of political "reflection.") For example, while the Democracy Fellows clearly would count keeping up with current events (an activity that the cohort group proclaimed as important and indicative of active citizenship) fellows' representations of that keeping-up process were much more thoughtful and nuanced. They spoke of "developing an open mind," "formulating my opinion on key social issues," "giving serious thought to specific ways that I can get involved," "becoming public minded"—much more taxing and formidable mental exercises and imaginative outcomes than simply watching and sorting through television commentary. Gastil and Dillard's (1999a and 1999b) research suggests that deliberation's cognitive and communicative exercise results in a general sophistication in political judgment. (See also, Burkhalter, Gastil, and Kelshaw 2002.) These advanced cognitive abilities generally manifested themselves over and over throughout the program in such other venues as assessing a deliberation, considering the hypothetical, evaluating the deliberative model, and critiquing their own performances.

Democracy Fellows were more efficacious in their political attitudes and language. The perceived lack of political efficacy on the part of young people has been widely documented (The Harwood Group 1993; Hays 1998; Owen 1997; Poole and Mueller 1998), and later we will address this important issue more explicitly. Our students were no exception, and many seemed to agree with this student statement from the 2001 Wingspread Conference: "Although many people think that college students have legitimacy to speak out and participate in politics (as we are the next in line to inherit power), some do not" (2001, 4). What is important in our finding is how deliberation appeared to affect efficacy, and in particular, the differences we noticed in how the students handled that absence of power to which many students attest.

Students in the cohort seemed resigned. To them political power at Wake Forest is elusive, determined by money, public relations, and decisions made "behind closed doors." They were incredulous that the Parents Council could get grilled cheese reinstated after it was removed from the cafeteria menu, when they, the students, were unable to do so. And they feared that political action could evoke retaliation. When asked what they thought would happen if students asked the administration for an accounting of financial matters, a cohort student said: "They would punish you!" Another student agreed: "Like I made a complaint to Residence Life and Housing this year and I already feel like they're going to give me the lowest number next semester because I bet they know my name. Like I guarantee it. I'll have a low housing number because of that." One cohort student even deemed political action "dangerous": "look what happened to the Dixie Chicks!"

Democracy Fellows, agreed that the administrators held the power seats on campus, but seemed not to be intimidated by them. Harkening back to the action imperative, one fellow insisted: "you have to work for a voice." To that end, they talked about actions such as getting to know the power brokers, engaging in political discussions with classmates and friends, building coalitions, and starting campus campaigns. Repeatedly, when faced with a question of power, Democracy Fellows more often than not, defaulted to more creative solutions that *imagined* them having power, rather than to the hopelessness (and voicelessness) that characterized the general Wake Forest student population in the 2005 HERI survey results described in Chapter Six. One fellow summed up the progression of efficacy that we noticed: "The longer I've been here, the more I feel like I can do something. I have more power than I want . . . most days."

Given the chilling comment of the Gonzaga student reported in the Harwood Study (1993)—"The one thing I learned, to be quite honest, is that I can't change anything"—our finding of a deliberative antidote is important. Over the course of the study, students often echoed their counterpart from Gonzaga, but ulti-mately, those who mastered deliberation skills, even those who were briefly exposed to them, came to sing a different tune. (See Burkhalter, Gastil, and Kelshaw 2002; Fishkin and Luskin 1999.)

Democracy Fellows were more communal in political language and outlook. Despite a robust tradition of American rugged individualism (Barber 1984; Rothwell 1998) which contextualizes American higher education, perhaps the most essential pedagogical move in teaching citizenship is to assist students in learning to think and speak communally (Hale 2001). Social psychology research suggests that opportunities, such as deliberation, for face-to-face discussion can contribute to more communal thinking (Delli Carpini, Cook, and Jacobs 2004). McMillan and Harriger (2002, 244) found that entering students possess an aversion to such attitudes because, as many of their citizen counterparts, they "fear that their individual interests may not be best served if left to the whims of collective decision-making." However, if students are to be reintroduced to the principles and responsibilities of the social contract (Flanagan 2003), excessive individualism is a con-cern. William Strauss, coauthor of *Millennials Rising: The Next Great Generation*, argues that those students born around 1982, the "millennials," are different from the previous Gen-X, in that they have more "collective confidence" more belief in the value of teamwork (Neary 2003). This is good news for democracy because not only can collectivism feed the very foundation of the system philosophically, it may translate practically into more grassroots and hands-on political action.

Our study of these Millennial students reflected some of the ambiguity one might expect in a transitional period, but, as the study progressed, there were decidedly more individualistic attitudes and language emanating from the comparison group and more communal references from the Democracy Fellows. As we noted in Chapter Six, when the senior cohort was asked to consider why they might engage in politics, they responded with a litany of self-interest (e.g., health care, Social Security, the economy). Each of these examples, of course, could be regarded as a community issue as well, but the cohort students used them as personal examples of why they might be persuaded to become politically active. One student put it plainly: "Politics must affect me directly to gain my interest." The Democracy Fellows, on the other hand, at the end of their intensive training in deliberative theory and practice started, not with individual pay-offs, but with the premise of individual responsibility: "The individual must accept the responsibility that comes with being a citizen"; "the time, energy, and interest must be present [in the individual] from the beginning"; "individuals themselves must change their own perspectives before their cynicism of politics will disappear." For the Democracy Fellows, that position remained largely intact and was reaffirmed in their final interviews concerning the importance of "community," or what David Mathews (1996) calls "public making"—choice work, widespread inclusion, common ground, voice, perspective taking—in short, as one fellow put it: "a better life for all."

Democracy Fellows were more imaginative in recognizing possibilities for deliberation and applying deliberative knowledge and skills to a broad range of situations. The attitude of the comparison group toward teaching deliberation in the service of citizenship was predictable, given their limited experience with it. The following comment typifies the lukewarm response to deliberation conveyed by students in the cohort: "It [deliberation] wouldn't hurt." Clearly, there were some enthusiastic students who recognized the need for deliberative skills and thought that "deliberation would work at Wake Forest." Some even recognized that the focus groups, which they admitted enjoying, were akin to this option, and they did almost uniformly agree with their Democracy Fellow counterparts about the value of politics as talk, especially in the classroom. However, they lodged many of the same complaints that they had of democratizing the campus: "takes too much time"; "won't produce action"; and "won't appeal to students."

The Democracy Fellows, on the other hand, were enthusiastic about the potential of the deliberative model (i.e., for increasing political engagement, leveling the playing field, creating alternatives). Perhaps most striking was the range of benefits the fellows attributed to their education in deliberation: deliberation training had made them better students; improved oral and written communication skills; abated their anxieties about speaking up in class, prepared them for job interviewing; trained them for leadership in clubs, fraternities, and church groups; and strengthened their interpersonal relationships through active listening and more careful responses.

While we rather expected that deliberation might improve attitudes about politics for students, the residuals of personal growth and development caught us by surprise. It should, however, be welcome news to the institution of higher education and its larger goals of developing—in any way that it can—the "whole" student and doing so "for life" (Dryzek 2000; Prince 2000).

Other students' limited exposure to deliberation on campus increased their political enthusiasm and optimism. Because the focus of this study was on sustained deliberative training and exposure and its effect on political development, this finding was somewhat surprising. Essentially, the data came from two sources: the student participants from the fall 2002 campus deliberation on community at Wake Forest and a few repeaters who attended no more than four focus groups.

First, as we reported in Chapter Four, we were unprepared for the unbridled enthusiasm of the deliberation participants: "really good to see a lot of students come out"; "impressed with the city showing"; "it [deliberation] is really valuable"; "this [the campus] is the perfect place for deliberation." Furthermore, the reaction of these one-timers was reflective as well as emotional. They spoke of diversity, the hearing of different points of view, efficacy, a level playing field, rational discussion, active listening, common ground —textbook claims by deliberation advocates, this time by students who had not been exposed to the theory. In short, the comments of student participants suggested that, not only did they find the campus deliberation enjoyable, they were able to identify skills that they saw in play, which would predict that they might be able to employ them in the future. Given the discouraging state of college student efficacy nationwide, perhaps one of our most important outcomes was the hopefulness that the campus deliberation engendered: "I think students will do things . . . with the results"; "this encouraged me to do things through my organization"; "in participating in the deliberation itself, I really saw the good that could come out of this."

Another surprising affirmation for ad hoc deliberation came in the final focus group when one member of the senior cohort praised the focus group itself as an opportunity to deliberate, and spontaneously described the essential power-building effects of deliberation:

> I've been here [in the cohort focus groups] since my freshman year. I enjoy coming. . . . I really do. I have my opinions, and . . . a lot of stuff is really important to me, and I like hearing, in this type of environment, what other people have to say. We are not here for a grade. You are not testing us on anything. . . . I feel like in a room of great people who know things about life, politics and everything else. They have opinions, and they are educated, and they care about, you know, living a good life and making the world a better place. . . . So I think, bouncing that off in a less competitive environment than a classroom would be beneficial, and . . . I know I am talking my head off.

The enthusiastic testimony of this senior aligns with the 2005 HERI data to suggest an unanticipated outcome of this study:

even a modicum of deliberative experience, less formal and less frequent, appears to expand civic preparation, or at least students' perceptions of it.

The Role of Context

The classroom offers knowledge and directed practice, but fails to simulate an authentic democratic environment. The students were right that the classroom offers the most comfortable venue in which to learn to deliberate; as teachers, we felt the same way. Even if, as London (2000, 15) reports, too little "discovery," "learning," and "engagement," actually happens in many classrooms, it is the case that we all know the ropes there. And we know the rules, which include who has the power of the grade and who wants a good one—the variables that too often trump all others. (See Freie 1997, for a discussion of a "contract" for deliberative study as opposed to a grade.) Based on that power differential, teachers can determine what essential knowledge about politics and deliberation is foundational for a solid citizen (Benhabib 1996), and students can be required to attend to that material. Teachers also have the prerogative to select some issue of keen interest, which puts political and deliberative theory into action (Loeb 1994, 97), and to oversee students as they "practice" democratic participation, safely and with minimal consequences. Because the risk is small, students can afford to express opinions, try on new attitudes, even rehearse civic behaviors as they craft their emerging civic personas (Campbell 2005). They can even dare to fail (Ervin 1997).

There are drawbacks, however. The classroom does not practice what it preaches about democracy. Given its cocoonlike quality, the classroom may be the farthest thing from the real world of political life, and students are quick to see the contradiction (Lauer 1994, 68). The disconnect was most apparent at the points of deliberation when participants sought to move from talk to action. (See Ryfe 2006, 84.) While they had little trouble identifying common ground between them, because students possessed no authentic political power to influence the issue-at-hand, they had great trouble projecting collective action. Furthermore, the classroom does not model the theoretical equality of the polity (Mitchell 1998). Even as they are taught and quickly come to praise the ability of deliberation to level the playing field, they recognize that in the classroom it is not so. According to Morse (1993), classroom equality must be based on respect for roles and ideas, because status and knowledge are inherently unequal. Students admit that because of the ultimate threat of a poor grade, they may posture and manage their class participation to court the favor of the teacher rather than engage in the raw, messy democratic process. The teachers have a wholly other conundrum: they must grapple with the requirement for neutrality as they simultaneously seek to direct learning and to teach toward improvement (Ryfe 2006, 89).

The campus develops organizing skills and enhances efficacy, but is still a limited democratic venue. Widening deliberative experimentation to the campus is an excellent opportunity for students to showcase deliberation—to demonstrate the breadth and utility of deliberative skills that they have learned and to engage an issue that is relevant and compelling to the campus community (O'Connell 1997). On the macro level, because student deliberators know the players and the physical space, logistical elements, such as planning, recruitment, and implementation, are relatively easy. Institutional support can likely be obtained as well because philosophically it would be unseemly for any campus authority figure to resist the students' right to assemble and discuss. On a micro level, there exists what Benhabib (quoted in Enslin, et al. 2001, 124) calls a "plurality of modes of association": clubs, organizations, fraternities, and sororities, which daily engage in decision-making processes, are likely to be open to learning and using the model. At its best, deliberation offers a significant antidote to the problem of student efficacy in that it has the potential to empower both the student deliberators and the wider campus population. Furthermore, a successful deliberation might even change attitudes and policy.

As a pedagogical venue, the campus is a bit more risky, however, because students must leave the "empathetic spaces" (Borowiec and Langerock 2002) of the classroom where the teacher and familiar classmates have shared their interests, corrected their mistakes, and buffered their political egos (Ervin 1997). Now they must convince other classmates, friends, and even campus power brokers of the importance of an issue and the ability of deliberation to address, even to solve, it. As in the classroom, on the campus "the norms of equality and symmetry are [also] necessarily restricted" (Enslin, et al. 2001, 124; Sanders 1997); in fact, in terms of shared governance, academic institutions may be among society's most entrenched hierarchies (Becker and Cuoto 1996). Because students are still subject to the direction and control of administrators, boards of trustees, and faculty, there are a limited number of issues over which students have any realistic influence or control, making the same leap from talk to action that troubled classroom deliberation in the campus venue as well (Cooper 2004).

The community exposes students to the messiness of democracy, but challenges their sense of efficacy. The community is a virtual treasure trove of rich learning experiences (Bringle and Hatcher 2002; Eyler and Giles 1999; McLeod, et al. 1999; Thomas 2003; Zlotkowski 1996, 1999); it is an authentic democratic environment, deals with substantive issues of community interest, presents a virtual clinic in community organizing and implementation, and offers an opportunity to connect the college and its host city in a meaningful way. However, from the vantage point of both college students and teachers, it is also the most difficult venue of all. As Edward Weeks discovered in his study of deliberative dialogue efforts in four cities, for an effective dialogue to take place "public participation must be broad, informed, deliberative, and credible" and such a process is "neither cheap, fast, nor easy" (2000, 369, 371).

Very few citizens from the community know the student organizers, or have any investment in their deliberative training. In our experience, students ultimately realized that their potential recruits for the community deliberation were real people, with real lives, jobs, and concerns—the people who students say they will be when they have time to be civically active. Furthermore, these community citizens would not consider coming out on a cold fall evening for anything less than a crucial social or political concern, widely heralded, and even then, the odds of a large and varied attendance are not good. There was a sense, however, that the issue of urban sprawl discussed in our community deliberation had real consequences—that it mattered. The students also never doubted that they were the face of their university—that if they studied, researched, and wrote about the issue well and grappled with it alongside these community members, it was likely that the participants would increase their regard for Wake Forest.

As we recounted in Chapter Five, the community deliberation the students organized was challenging, certainly relative to the other two venues that they had experienced. First, while the issue of urban sprawl had seemed a relevant one initially, and one that certainly increased local knowledge for the Democracy Fellows as they researched and wrote about it, they learned a critical lesson about issues and timing. A series of events—notably an annexation battle—came and went between the time the issue book was begun and the deliberation was held. What was very important in spring 2003, may have seemed less so to citizens in the fall. Students also underestimated the time and initiative that off-campus preparations would require, i.e., site selection and affordability, access, and transportation of people and materials. Accustomed to access in the campus newspaper, e-mail network, and easy campus signage, students also found publicity for this communitywide event to be difficult. Their most significant failure, however, happened in the area of recruiting. Mistakenly buoyed by their ability in the campus context to call upon classmates, friends, faculty members, and sympathetic administrators, students were daunted by the difficulty of coaxing community citizens—especially a diverse cross-section—to attend. (See McLeod, et al. 1999, for the impact of size and heterogeneity of the deliberation on political participation.)

The deliberation process itself offered some lessons as well. Though, for the most part, student moderators appeared to have functioned well, some were unprepared for tough questions from participants about the inevitability of sprawl, the complexity of the issue, and whether citizen discussion could really change anything. As we have reported, one moderator virtually lost control of his group when a city councilman launched a filibuster of sorts and other annoyed participants retaliated. Some students reported that they felt powerless and somewhat condescended to—that in some ways, the community seemed to be enabling the students' "little project"—not at all the perspective or the intent of the students. This perception occurred chiefly when students sought to refocus on the NIF model of deliberation when participants clearly wanted just to talk. Community participants, however, clearly appreciated the students' work on the issue book, demonstrated by the fact that most participants had read it and came prepared to talk. Many of the students reciprocated with a newfound interest in, and concern for, their community.

All of the contexts presented faculty role conflicts, but the community was the most challenging. Throughout the study, we struggled with our roles (Harriger and McMillan 2005). In the first two deliberative venues, we faced tensions between the roles of teacher, moderator, and researcher as we have outlined earlier; in the community venue, two additional roles added to the tension: those of administrator and citizen. In retrospect, the students needed far more direction in conducting the proceedings than we had anticipated. They needed greater delineation of duties, scheduling, and adherence to a timeline. They needed concrete suggestions for publicity and follow-up accountability. They needed realistic, explicit goals for recruiting. And most of all they needed more psychological and emotional preparation for the gloves-off, no-holds-barred arena of real public discussion and some practical strategies they might employ to deal with these difficulties if they arose. In short, while we as instructors had to take responsibility for our own administrative shortcomings, we remained convinced that the community deliberation with its authenticity, opportunities for community organizing, appreciation of an important local issue, and bridging the town/gown divide afforded the students some of the most important lessons of this project.

Finally, we also felt compromised in our roles as citizens, although, in fairness, we saw this one coming. (See McKee 2004.) As we witnessed breaches in the arrangements and warning signs that recruitment was not going well, we asked ourselves: "Do we move to rescue the situation?" or "Do we trust the process and allow our students to experience whatever outcome this deliberation yields?" In Chapter Five we explained the middle-ground that we opted for, but it was not a totally comfortable place to stand. In fact, of the various role tensions a project such as this presents, balancing teacher and citizen simultaneously was clearly the most challenging.

The Influence of the College Experience

Early political socialization is critical to robust and ongoing civic awareness and action. While there are conflicting views in the literature about how to engage the political energy and participation of young people (Gibson 2001), there is virtual consensus that the process starts early. In fact, some, including some of our Democracy Fellows, argue that to start these efforts in college may be too late. Around the dinner table, in the elementary classroom, volunteering in the community or accompanying their parents as they do so— youngsters are exposed to opportunities to develop civic competence (Youniss, McLellan, and Yates 1997): to learn how the government functions, how to participate, and how to cooperate in collective decision making and other social action. Flanagan (2003, 258) suggests that such early exposure to the social world outside themselves allows young people "to see their interests realized in the interests of the whole." So it did not surprise us that when asked about how their political socialization occurred, one freshman fellow remarked that "people are very much a result of their circumstances." He echoed the accounts of several other Democracy Fellows when they recalled dinner-table conversation about politics; interactions with parents and other relatives concerning politics; participation in the campaign of a local politician; engaged classrooms; and experiences, such as debate, model legislatures, model UN, or serving as a page or intern for a legislative body. Some students developed their political enthusiasm despite, or perhaps in reaction to, a politically inactive household, an unenthusiastic teacher, or the widely reported disappointment with student government, which one student labeled "pointless . . . a popularity contest." One Democracy Fellow entered our program with limited exposure to politics. She thought she "didn't have much to offer," but caught fire politically and by the end of her matriculation had distinguished herself as an intern and researcher at the Kettering Foundation.

The importance of early exposure to politics was not revealed in the Democracy Fellows alone. Students in the cohort who reported a strong interest in politics and active participation spoke of the same sorts of robust pre-college influences that many of the Democracy Fellows claimed. These student reports reinforced for us the conclusion of scholars in the field of youth socialization who have determined that civic training in adolescence can have a real impact on adult civic behavior and the development of competencies (McLellan and Youniss 1997; Verba, Schlozman, and Brady 1995). Many also believe that it is the combination of school, family, and community factors that make up the most positive political socialization experience (Andolina, Jenkins, Zukin, and Keeter 2003). Our study clearly suggests, however, that despite early influences, the college years are not too late to influence civic commitment and that higher education still has a critical role to play (Pascarella and Terenzini 2005).

College students have high hopes that college will prepare them for citizenship but are not sure how or what they are willing to do to contribute to the process. This is quite a profound finding. As higher-education experts and civic-education advocates are busily debating whether college and universities should be about the business of citizenship training (see, for example, Barber 2001; Boyte 2001; Colby, et al. 2003; Englund 2002; Gamson 2000; Walker 2002; Zarefsky 1993), someone forgot to ask the students. Actually, nowhere in the literature we reviewed was the question put to the students, so we decided to include it. Overwhelmingly, our student respondents—both those in the Democracy Fellows program and their peers—reflected the sentiment of this fellow:

Universities should work to train students how to be active citizens in society. . . . [They] cannot even hope to produce freethinking, independent, politically responsible citizens without bestowing the skills and practice necessary. The university, serving as a model for democracy, could produce powerful change.

While this sentiment, which persisted throughout the four years of matriculation for these students, sounds eloquent and hopeful, it was accompanied by a measure of ambivalence, even abdication (Hays 1998). Students seemed uncertain about how they wanted to receive this training—in particular, about what they thought would be the most effective way to make active citizens of themselves and their classmates. They noted that the structure is already in place to deliver citizenship training in the classroom (Ervin 1997; Morse 1993), and many saw that venue as especially helpful in learning the basics of political theory and research. However, most considered the classroom, especially the traditional monologic, lecture methods, as "boring," "passive," and "ineffective." (See London's 2000 report of higher-education professionals who used synonymous terms.) Many students liked the idea of democratizing the campus as an institutional model for civic learning (Carey 2000; Morse 1993) but doubted that they were up to the responsibility of carrying their weight. Most students were realistic about the level of maturity, experience, and commitment that it would take for them to be substantially involved in campus decision making, and one respondent worried that students might not "show up to govern" unless the exercise were accompanied by "free food."

There were two options that were regarded favorably by the students: community service and teaching deliberative skills. Community service appealed because it was active—it got them out of the classroom and into the community where they could better see the fruits of their labors (Cooper 2004). They were consistent, however, in qualifying the conditions under which they would recommend a service component: the program must be executed well and students must not be required to take part. Finally, students liked the idea of teaching citizenship through deliberative skills and practice. Although we cannot be sure how much of this favor derived from the fact that most of them knew the general nature of our research, it is certainly the case that throughout the interviews and focus groups, they talked about how much they prefer classes where the central mode is discussion —in which they are allowed to express their opinions and to hear others (Campbell 2005; Ervin 1997; Walker 2002; Young 2000).

The good news then is that college students expect to exit their institutions as active citizens and most likely will cooperate with this institutional goal. The bad news is that they almost expect it to happen by magic. Given the fact that they are "too busy" to engage in substantial citizenship right now and the rather intractable conditions that they place on the options of delivering citizenship, one suspects that they are hoping for some version of "citizenship lite," that will be relatively painless to receive, but nearby and available for future use should they want to exercise the option.

Despite a basic belief in the soundness of the American political system, college students are turned off by politics-as-usual. Just prior to the turn of the century, Carol Hays in her analysis of young Americans' regard for politics delivered the troubling news that *alienation*—a catchall term that includes cynicism, distrust, lack of efficacy, and apathy—was the "most widespread characterization of this generation" (1998, 45). As we reported at the beginning of our study, we sat and watched with the Democracy Fellows as the terror attacks of 9/11 changed all that, and for a time at least, cast a halo effect over our students' regard for the political system of their country. Right after the attacks, our students, like many interviewed at Michigan State University, shared the sentiment that Nancy Lange (2002, 21) reported in that study: "I have never been so proud to be an American." This basic belief in the soundness of the system persisted throughout the tenure of these students. One student opined: "I just see it [the political system] working like the founders wanted it to." Another even reframed voter apathy as evidence of the effectiveness of the political system: "The main goal of politics is running our country and if the general public is content . . . it can't be doing too much too wrong." However, as their education progressed, student critiques became more thoughtful, and they especially seemed moved by the power of contrast. Students repeatedly recounted stories of travel and study-abroad experiences in countries where they witnessed very different ways of doing the people's business.

From the beginning, students cited particular characteristics of the political system that worried them and many of these offenders did not change. For example, throughout the course of the project they railed most fervently against the stranglehold of partisanship, a sentiment that apparently is widely shared by their peers. A *Newsweek* poll reported that most young people view the two-party system as "irrelevant, corrupt or worse" (Fineman 2000, 26). Ted Halstead, president of the New America Foundation and author of *The Radical Center: The Future of American Politics* suggested to Lynn Neary of National Public Radio that the single fact that most unites young voters is their rejection of the two-party system: "Never have we seen generations so keen to identify themselves as Independents" (July 14, 2003). Wake Forest students also were consistent in their belief that money drives politics and offers an unfair advantage to those who control it. A nationwide survey of young people reports a similar finding: 71 percent believe that political candidates would rather talk to older, wealthier people than to younger ones (Center for Information and Research on Civic Learning and Engagement 2002). This concern for the role of money in politics resurfaced in virtually every interview cycle through students' persistent interest in campaign finance reform. Finally, students seemed truly disheartened by their inability to get what they consider to be reliable political information. One young woman offered a true dot-com lament for her generation:

> I can go online and get as much research as I want, but I can't find anything not based on someone's opinion about one candidate or the other, and I can look at one issue and get two completely different answers. . . . I just want to get the facts and make my own opinion.

Students have an efficacy problem, which does not abate over the four years; it just shifts. There is no news in the proposition that young people feel powerless where politics is concerned (The Harwood Group 1993; Hays 1998; Owen 1997) and that this lack of efficacy has both external dimensions (social institutions, especially government, do not solve problems or work for the people) and internal dimensions ("I can't change anything with my vote") (Center for Information and Research on Civic Learning and Engagement 2002; Poole and Mueller 1998). The reasons why students are turned off by politics—excessive partisanship, the power and influence of money, and the elusiveness of reliable political information—all reveal an underlying sense of powerlessness.

Efficacy persisted as a major construct throughout this study as well, with students citing the war in Iraq, the botched 2000 election in Florida, poor campaign finance reform, media overreach, and confusion over political issues and facts, as examples of both internal and external inefficacy. What appears to have happened in our study around this issue, however, is twofold: 1) students identified and, in some cases, attempted to tap external power sources closer to home (i.e., the administration, faculty, the community), and 2) through the deliberative experience, Democracy Fellows (and even one-time deliberators) became more acutely aware of their own personal efficacy, or lack thereof.

Over the course of the study, all student participants portrayed the administration as the most powerful political actor on campus, followed by faculty, parents and alums, and some few influential students, with the average Wake Forest student clearly in last place. "Getting the ear" of the more influential groups—as one student put it: "just badgering and more badgering"—translates to power. Most students were willing to admit, however, that on campus they had "about as much power as they were willing to exercise." What is most striking about this external attribution of power is its persistence from beginning to end in this study; students seem habitually aware of the locus of power and their relationship to it in every social situation (Pfeffer and Salancik 1974). What started out in initial interviews as remote power attributions—political parties, the federal government, and the media—which students were unable to influence, migrated to campus power brokers, often perceived as equally inaccessible. Though efficacy expanded and became more recognizable for the Democracy Fellows, students across groups established political accountability outside themselves, and did so routinely.

A second interesting finding concerns the way in which deliberation highlights and mediates efficacy for those students who experience it. Power was perhaps *the* central concept discussed by students (17 of them to be exact) in their final first-year seminar papers. These texts reflected that students were particularly attracted to Benjamin Barber's contention (1999, 35) that "deliberation without power is a fraud." Fellows wrote about how learning and practicing deliberation had revealed the truth of Barber's quote. They spoke of becoming empowered by being able to express their opinions, learning the most effective and efficacious ways to do so, and by having adequate knowledge with which to participate. They also spoke about their feelings of disempowerment when they were in the minority, knew less than others did about an issue, or, as one writer put it: "As students, [we] felt that we had no control over the problem, and therefore had little motivation to act."

Clearly, the Democracy Fellows came to understand the concerns about the intersection of power and deliberation (see, for example, Bohman 1996; Dryzek 2000; Mouffe 1999; Young 1996, 1997), because they experienced some of those concerns themselves. In earlier findings we demonstrated how facing and exposing the fraudulent potential of deliberation actually came to increase the efficacious attitudes and language of the Democracy Fellows. Even for those students who experienced deliberation only one time or for some repeat focus group participants, power was writ large and seemed to reveal to students both deliberation's empowering and disempowering potential.

Political knowledge matters. It is not news that the role of political knowledge has been, over time, a contested notion (Dudley and Gitelson 2003). Today's citizens know about as much as they did 50 years ago, despite the existence of markedly more general knowledge and more education (Constructing Civic Virtue: A

Symposium on the State of American Citizenship 2003). Some people temper this disappointing news with the argument that we do not need much knowledge to make political decisions (Popkin 1991). Delli Caprini and Keeter (1996) improved the debate by shifting the emphasis from quantity to quality. They asked the critical question, what difference does knowledge make? This question has particular resonance in the classroom where a teacher continually grapples with the tension between how much foundational material to deliver (usually through lectures) and how much to let students discover on their own (often through discussions). Our study affirms that both methods are critical, but that successful deliberation invariably starts with a sound knowledge base.

Democracy Fellows consistently echoed the thought expressed by one of their number that "in this short time span of the deliberative democracy class . . . I have learned more about the history and basic ideas about democracy than I have in the rest of my life." While evidence of acquired knowledge surfaced in both the interviews and the focus group transcripts, we were able to see that those students who had course exposure to politics and democratic theory were able to talk about them more knowledgeably and to apply them more appropriately than were those who had not had the same exposure.

Initially, we attributed this advanced political knowledge and utility solely to the fellows' intensive first-year seminar experience. It is important to note that the NIF model by which the Democracy Fellows were trained incorporates a baseline of common knowledge for all deliberation participants in the form of the issue book. (See Mathews and McAfee 2000; Ryfe 2006, 93), so that no one enters the discussion ignorant of the issue. In addition, however, fellows talked of how knowledge was formed and expanded in the process of the discussion itself, eventually morphing from personal to public knowledge. As one student put it:

> When I entered a deliberation, I possessed a personal knowledge of the issue, yet by temporarily putting aside my view and listening to others' stories, I gained a public knowledge about racial and ethnic tensions and about public education that I never would have had alone.

The structural advantages of the Deliberative Democracy class led us to conclude initially that the first-year seminar accounted for the difference in political knowledge that we observed in the data. Over time, however, we realized that there were differences in political knowledge—spoken and applied—even among the students in the cohort. Upon careful reflection, we were able to see that those students who had taken political science courses were more like the Democracy Fellows in political knowledge and verbal application than they were like their fellow classmates in the cohort (Gimpel, Lay, and Schuknecht 2003)—offering at least one empirical example of the fact that knowledge matters. It would be a mistake to conclude that the process of deliberation offers some watered down version of civic acumen which substitutes for the solid knowledge transfer of the traditional lecture. Rather our study suggests that the two pedagogical forms— lecture and discussion—might work best in tandem.

College students do not see themselves as political activists now, but speak of deferring that responsibility to a "less busy time" of their lives. Concerns about the alienation of young people from politics have been widely documented (Clymer 2000; Delli Carpini and Keeter 1996; The Harwood Group 1993; Johnson, Hays, and Hays 1998), and reasons for that disconnect have been explored. What this study brings into sharp relief, however, is how college students in particular rationalize their political inactivity— what they tell themselves about their relationship to politics and whether those messages can be modified or reversed.

Our participation surveys beginning in the sophomore year revealed, at least among the Democracy Fellows, a relatively high percentage of traditional political action measures, such as voting, reading the newspaper, or writing one's congressperson. Very early in our data gathering, we also noticed a curious but prominent theme that we began to call, with linguistic assistance from Martin Luther King Jr., "citizenship deferred." (See also, Campus Compact 2002; Loeb 1994, 114.) The concept seemed to have two distinct supporting tenets: 1) college students are "too busy"—with extracurricular and social lives, but especially with academics—

to engage in or even give serious, sustained attention to political activity, and 2) politics is for students in specific disciplines.

The students we talked to constructed a rationale for postponing political activity that was plausible and apparently widely shared: that during college they were somehow civic apprentices who must "defer [civic responsibility] to some continually receding future" (Loeb 1994, 114). They explain their deferment this way: college students come from high-school environments where they were "top dogs"—both academically and socially—and where they "have time to do everything." Perhaps that favorable status buffers them from intensive study and allows more leisure for extracurricular and social activities. Now they find themselves experiencing a culture shock (Astin 1993; Levine and Cureton 1998; Pascarella and Terenzini 1991), which often takes the form of what one student called "an academic awakening," surrounded by peers who are "just as smart or smarter than you are," and competing for what students seem to regard as the elusive *A*, as well as for social status on campus. Additionally, there is a plethora of interesting activities that compete for their time and allegiance. As one student put it: "It is humbling" and over-whelming, and it allows little time for serious political reflection, much less action. Another student highlighted the choices thus: "Here you're like, protest or study for my next test? I think I might want to study."

Citizenship is more accessible, students allow, if one is taking courses, in subjects like political science or sociology or education, in which social and political issues are indigenous to the discipline and therefore, front and center. As one student observed: "I think it depends on what classes you take too because I've been in like these biology classes where it's like yeah, what was there [politi-cally] to talk about?" Apparently, it is hard for students to imagine politics-across-the-curriculum, and even more troubling, how political decisions penetrate even the most unlikely places of everyday life. Furthermore, because of their "busyness," college students conclude that "acting [politically] later on will be easier" (Loeb 1994, 114).

Catalysts for political action clustered around certain definitive elements, but often with opposite effects. Students were very clear and consistent over the four years about the things that encouraged them to engage in civic action and those that did not. Furthermore, this is one category in which there was only a negligible difference between the Democracy Fellows and the cohort, a convergence that is reflected in national trends. (See, for example, Andolina et al. 2003; Gibson 2001; Sherrod, Flanagan, and Youniss 2002.) For Wake Forest students those catalysts for political action mentioned most often were classes, the inspiration of a teacher/mentor, the opportunity to study abroad, local campus issues, and national political issues. What was most striking about this list, however, is that many times the same event caused diametrically opposite reactions in our student respondents.

Because many of these catalysts have been discussed elsewhere in this book, we offer here two cases in which a single event functioned to encourage one student toward political activism and to discourage another. The mid-term elections of 2002, in which Arnold Schwarzenegger was elected governor of California, spurred one budding activist in our focus group to increase his political participation. He explained:

> Since I'm a really big cynic and a blooming liberal, I kind of see it as like you know . . . signs of the apocalypse . . . the Cubs and Red Sox were in the World Series . . . Arnold's in office, and I don't know, I'm just glad he was born in Austria and can't be president. But no, it just reinforces my constant cynicism in the way that our politics is run. . . . Makes me want to get involved to a certain extent.

The same election had the opposite effect on another student: "I'm to the point that I'm not going to pick up the paper any more. I just don't care. . . . I'm just tired of hearing dumb people say dumb things, whether it's nationally or whether it is in the OGB [the campus newspaper]."

Another issue that galvanized students was what we all came to refer to as "the *Howler* incident." The school yearbook for 2001-2002, the *Howler*, was distributed as students were departing campus after spring semester of 2002. Yearbook writers had offered an opinion on the previous fall's election of Homecoming king and queen, which some thought had racist overtones. Because students had summer vacation to read and assess yearbook content, the fireworks were deferred until the fall of 2002 as returning students lined up on all sides of the issue. Some felt that the portrayal of an African American queen as being unrepresentative of the student population was racially insensitive; others thought that yearbook writers had merely stated a cultural truth; still others considered the whole issue to be much ado about nothing. Remedies included everything from pasting an alternative text on top of the offending one to cutting the page out of every single shiny new yearbook. More substantive approaches, however, sought to get at the root of the alleged offense to examine race relations on the Wake Forest campus. Some students with whom we talked that fall called the controversy "ridiculous" and a political disincentive. But others disagreed:

> [I] mean if someone thinks this [the *Howler* piece] is like an important issue that impacts something they're really involved in, I think they will really act and speak out on something they think is important. But I think it's really hard to say; hey, this issue is important.

This student was impressed by the courage of those who sought to initiate dialogue, in particular a campuswide forum, over a substantive issue, and he reported that for him their courage was contagious. Young (2000, 50) acknowledges that the "field of struggle is not level," but that students can learn by observing "fair, open, and inclusive democratic processes [as they] attend to such disadvantage."

We heard the same kind of ambivalence over classes and the influence, either positive or negative, of teachers. As we have reported, students were quick to praise classes in which professors welcomed queries and diverse opinions and students were encouraged "to think for themselves." They were very critical, on the other hand, when they felt that professors used the power of their rank and the student's grade to proselytize or intimidate in order to reinforce the professor's pedagogical agenda or point of view. Students seem to sense the presence of what Ruth Grant calls an "ethics of talk" in the classroom, which at its best fosters "crucial civic capacities" (1996, 7), but at its worst, diminishes civic enthusiasm and the desire to participate.

CHAPTER EIGHT

The Role of Higher Education

Chapter Eight

The Role of Higher Education

Much of our analysis thus far has been descriptive—explaining what we did in the Democracy Fellows program and what we found through interviews and focus groups with the fellows and their class cohorts. Here we take a prescriptive turn and discuss what we consider to be the implications of our findings for the role of higher education in preparing students for democratic citizenship.

There is considerable energy and talk in higher-education circles around the issues of civic engagement—some have even described it as a "movement" taking root, not only in higher education, but in other institutions and communities as well (Boyte 1980, 2001). But if we have learned anything in the last four years, it is this: encouraging active citizenship in college students is hard work and it must be done intentionally, thoughtfully, and carefully (Ryfe 2006). In many ways, such work may seriously challenge the received practices of higher education. In the end, a deep commitment to changing the perceptions of students of themselves asdemocratic citizens will require changing the perceptions of faculty and administrators of themselves and of their institutions.

As mentioned previously, Wake Forest makes much of its motto "*Pro Humanitate*"; the phrase is emblazoned on banners and mugs; it is emphasized often at Founders' Day, graduation, and other celebratory events; and it is used repeatedly in recruiting and viewbook rhetoric to remind prospective and current students that education at Wake Forest is education "in service of humankind." Indeed, all student respondents in our study reported a "strong service climate" on the campus, and the participation surveys consistently reflected that students were engaging in community service as well. What Wake Forest and many other institutions have not done as well, according to Colby, et al. (2000, xxvii), is to construct and implement "a coherent institutional strategy to implement those statements," especially one that ties service directly to the broader responsibilities of citizenship.

The university has not considered in a thoughtful, programmatic way what concepts and skills students need to become committed, active citizens, nor have we considered together the curriculum as a vehicle of citizenship. Tacitly then, we have not reinforced the notion that citizenship can be taught (O'Connell and McKenzie 1995; Pateman 1970). Put another way, we have failed to offer an alternative to what William Sullivan (2000, 21) calls the pedagogical "default option" of "instrumental individualism" which "leaves the larger issues of social, political and moral purpose out of explicit consideration." Instead, like many other colleges and universities, we have proclaimed our motto as if every campus citizen should understand it, and as if students will learn its requirements and responsibilities by osmosis. This is not to say that civic training does not happen on the Wake Forest campus but when it has occurred it has been because individual teachers and programs have fueled the flames of citizenship and service in their own disciplines (Ostrander 2004, 84). Service learning at Wake Forest began in this same way but has increasingly gained institutional support and, consequently, its impact has broadened.

Neither do we appear to recognize the modeling potential of our own campus governance (Carey 2000; Morse 1993; Thomas 2000, 66). Students report that one thing that turns them off to politics generally is the fact that what they are learning in their classes about democracy is not always consonant with what they observe in campus decision making (McMillan 2004). They often feel like a disenfranchised minority, even about issues that concern them. While they are realistic about their limitations in handling administrative power, the contradictions concerning equality, participation, and voice, are not lost on them.

Finally, despite the fact that Wake Forest has a long and storied history of tackling tough social and political issues, (e.g., evolution, freedom of speech, academic freedom, and autonomy) what the university and most of its academic counterparts have done less well is shouldering those same kinds of issues in partnership with their host communities. (See Bringle and Hatcher 2002; Brisbin and Hunter 2003.) In the issue book that the Democracy Fellows wrote for the campus deliberation, they described their campus as "its own little universe" physically isolated and "buffered" from the political and social struggles of their neighbors (Democracy Fellows 2002, 9). The students suggested that their civic education and that of future generations of Wake Foresters might be incomplete until the university reconsiders what Fogelman (2001) terms "its institutional commitment to public purposes and responsibilities" of those citizens in closest proximity to them.

In thinking about how to do the intentional work of nurturing democratic citizenship, it strikes us that there are both philosophical and programmatic considerations. Philosophical considerations relate to the larger motivating values and ideas that drive the work. When certain ideas become popular in higher education—as citizen engagement has become—then the rush to do something in that area accelerates, often leading to programs and expenditures that are not well thought out either with regard to motivating values or desired outcomes. The potential consequences range from having little impact to having a negative impact on students' motivations to become engaged citizens. Philosophical prescriptions argue that colleges and universities should spend some time thinking about what they are doing and why they are doing it before they embark on citizen-engagement projects. Programmatic considerations relate to the more practical implications of how to establish a program in civic engagement, once there is clarity on the values questions. On this subject, we learned much from our experience, both in terms of what seems to work and what does not. Our goal in sharing those experiences is to minimize the stumbling blocks for others and to maximize the positive effects we found in the program.

Philosophical Considerations

What is the purpose of higher education? Is it to transfer and create knowledge? Is it to equip students with a particular set of professional skills, which will enable them to succeed at their chosen endeavors? Is it to develop human beings who are concerned for others, committed to a notion of the public interest, and who embrace democratic values? Most colleges and universities identify all three of these purposes in their mission statements (Furco 2006). The history of the development of higher education in the United States, whether it be the creation of church-related, private, liberal arts schools, such as our own, or state, land-grant universities, is a story imbued with the notion of developing citizens for the emerging democracy (Barber 1998; Civic Engagement Task Force 2002; Fogleman 2001). Nonetheless, a survey of the wide variety of institutions today—public, private, large, small, two-year, four-year, graduate research, church-related, secular—would reveal that there is a wide variety of ways in which institutions approach these purposes and give them priority in the actual allocation of resources. Benjamin Barber (1998, 230) suggests that the movement away from the civic mission in higher education began by the beginning of the twentieth century and that by the end of WWII, "higher education had begun to professionalize and vocationalize and specialize in a manner that occluded its civic and democratic mission. Rights and responsibilities were decoupled and citizenship relegated to the occasional boring 'civics' lecture." The driving force behind the new civic-engagement movement is the notion that institutions of higher education should recover their civic mission and become actively engaged in the nurture of democratic values in their students (Colby, et al. 2000; London 2000). As Barber (1998, 230) argues, "lawyers and doctors are no more likely to make good citizens than dropouts if their training is limited to the narrow and self-interested world defined by vocational preparation and professional instruction."

Which values: politics or service? Even if one would achieve consensus that the university is in the business of value formation, the ability to reach agreement on what those values should be can prove to be even more challenging, particularly when they have political implications. In a time of highly polarized politics that have spilled into the ivory tower, it is not just citizens who shy away from entering the debate—institutions dependent on diverse donor bases, faculty concerned about tenure and outside watchdog groups, and administrators trying to keep the peace understandably worry about the ramifications of being "political." The consequence of this avoidance, however, is to leave students without guidance for what it means to be the enlightened citizen that their university's mission statement promises and to imply that politics is just one more specialization in the university, a subject for those who major in political science. It is our contention that the avoidance of defining citizenship in political terms, when talking about what democratic citizenship requires, has contributed to the growth of disengagement and alienation from the political process.

One way that some colleges and universities have attempted to address this dilemma is through a focus on community service. This is not to suggest that effectively integrating service into university life is easy, or that it does not invite controversy, but rather that it has become a substitute in some way for an emphasis on political citizenship (Long 2002), and at a cost. There has been an enormous increase in the amount of community service young people do both in high school and college, and the service-learning movement has become the vanguard for the civic-education movement in the academic arena (Barber and Battistoni 1993; Rimmerman 2005). There is a burgeoning literature on service and its impact on the development of young people and much to recommend it as a means of teaching compassion and understanding. (For a review of this literature, see Galston 2003.) But there is also mounting evidence that service, rather than being a stepping-stone to politics, can often act as a replacement for political engagement: "Without structured and informed reflection on the political implications of student service and the related issues of inequality and power," writes Richard Cuoto, "human needs in community service could metamorphose into 'feel good' efforts that conveyed false impressions to students" (1996, 82). Robert Putnam (2000) documents the precipitous decline in multiple measures of political engagement among young people at the same time that he finds increases in community service. Our own findings suggest that many of the students in the senior cohort preferred service to politics and remained largely unreflective about notions of the public interest, democracy, and public policy.

What kind of democracy? Our findings show that an emphasis on the political nature of citizenship can be successfully pursued and can have a positive impact on developing the democratic sensibilities of young people. But choosing to focus on the politics of citizenship does not end the decision making about how to teach civic engagement. There are competing notions in democratic theory about what democratic citizenship looks like and each vision suggests a different approach to teaching it. The dominant paradigm in American political science, and, one might add, in our current political culture, has been a notion of self-interested citizens whose motivation to act—or not—depends on whether they perceive their particular interests to be threatened. In this view, the public interest is simply the accumulation of multiple private interests and only minimal citizen participation is required, or even desirable. In essence, this kind of politics accepts the notion that only some people are actually interested in politics and that democracy is simply a process by which elites compete for the votes of only partially engaged citizens (Berelson, et al. 1954; Dahl 1956; Sartori 1962). Barber calls this "thin" democracy (1984).

Much of what passes for education in political citizenship today conforms to this vision of democracy: Provide the students who are interested with knowledge about how the system operates; explain how parties and interest groups compete to have their interests represented; encourage students to work in campaigns for candidates who reflect their interests; and emphasize voting as the key way they can protect their interests. The fact that most students are uninterested and disengaged from politics is not troubling if this elite notion of democracy is the model. The major mode of communication among citizens in this vision is debate: competing interests marshal evidence to support their preferred policy outcome and the two sides go at it, producing winners and losers depending upon the ability to persuade others to see their interests as yours.

However accurately this vision of democracy reflects reality (and this too is in some dispute), it seems clear that it is a vision of politics increasingly unappealing to citizens of all ages, but particularly to young people (Bennett 1997; Campus Compact 2002; Dionne Jr. 1991; Greider 1992; Harwood 1993; Hayes 1998; Levine and Curton 1998). In our research we found that members of our senior cohort, simply as a consequence of gaining a college education and following a presidential election on television, were likely to articulate this version of democratic citizenship. If an institution chooses to embrace what Barber calls thin democracy, there is not a great deal of change or intervention necessary. It will be enough to prepare students for citizenship by offering them courses in American government, training them in the skills of debate, and encouraging them to pay attention to elections and to vote. Many colleges and universities are already doing these things and the increase in turnout among young people in the 2004 election (Patterson 2004; Young 2004) suggests that, to some extent, it may be working.

There is however an alternative vision of politics that is more communal in nature and that motivates the civic-engagement movement. The theory that underlies the Democracy Fellows program and the choice to use deliberation as the mechanism for teaching political citizenship argues that democratic citizenship should move beyond immediate self-interest toward public-spiritedness and concern for others, and that participation in democratic institutions *outside* of the political arena can educate citizens for participation *in* that arena (Barber 1984; Becker and Couto 1996; Boyte 1989; Pateman 1970). Patrick (2000) captures this notion of citizenship when he writes about the development in students of democratic "dispositions" defined as the promotion of the general welfare, recognition of the common humanity of each person, respecting and protecting rights, taking responsibility for one's participation and supporting democratic principles and practices. It is not enough to teach students how the system operates and how to operate in it. Knowledge and skills are necessary but not sufficient if higher education is to help restore civic life in this country. The mode of communication in this view of democratic citizenship is necessarily something more than polarized debate. If people are to move beyond self-interest and come to understand their fellow citizens, they must develop listening as well as speaking skills, the capacity to explore the underlying values in policy preferences, the ability to recognize the ways in which each policy choice one makes involves trade-offs and the desire to seek common ground for action with others. As our results indicate, deliberation is an antidote to polarized debate. It is a model of democratic talk that has at its base the employment of reason in the pursuit of common understanding and the assumption of equality among those participating (Arnett and Arneson 1999; Mathews 1999). It can be taught—in fact, must be taught because it is a countercultural way of talking (McMillan and Harriger 2002)—and can be employed in most of the venues where learning occurs at colleges and universities. Our findings show that teaching this approach to democratic talk can inculcate students with the democratic dispositions of citizenship. An institutional commitment to using deliberation as a teaching method in the classroom and the primary method of discussion in campus life could have a substantial impact on developing a much wider cadre of citizens with these democratic dispositions.

The consequences of philosophical choices. Choosing this approach to democratic education does not end the philosophical challenges—in fact, it increases them. We discovered as we implemented the Democracy Fellows program that approaching democratic citizenship in this manner created real challenges to our established modes of teaching and doing research (Harriger and McMillan 2005), and for our students in their assessment of, and satisfaction with, their education and campus life. Encouraging students to think about democracy in the abstract and to apply it in their lives leads them to question issues of power, not just in the larger political world, but in the classroom and on the campus. Students valued classes where the deliberation and discussion of difficult issues was encouraged, but they noticed how few of these opportunities presented themselves. They also noticed when professors used their position in the classroom to impose their views on the class and they recognized the power imbalance and the discouragement of participation that it engendered. They watched debates on campus issues and understood when they had influence and when they did not. They became, in fact, critical thinkers about the power dynamics of campus life as they compared an ideal of democratic citizenship to the realities of their lives. We see these as positive developments—after all, should it not be our goal to create critical thinkers who know how to apply abstract concepts to their world? There are many campus venues where that ideal can actually be practiced. But to get there, colleges and universities must be willing to reflect on the messages they send students about democracy on their own campuses, and they must be willing to regard critiques from students as evidence of success rather than as random static to be ignored or stifled.

Finally, a commitment to preparing students for democratic citizenship requires universities to rethink their role in the communities they inhabit (Brisbin and Hunter 2003; Pew Partnership 2004) and to examine the concept of university-as-citizen (McMillan 2004). The broader community can be the best laboratory of all for students to develop their civic capacities, but sending them into the community unprepared to deal with diverse populations or complex public problems is to do both the students and the community a disservice (Cuoto 1996; Harriger and McMillan 2005). Town/gown problems are age-old, but problems that result from the isolation of the campus from the community probably cause less harm than problems that arise from exploiting the community for pedagogical purposes. Taking seriously the notion of the university itself as a citizen of the broader community, on the other hand, can produce substantial benefit both to the university and the community.

At the start, then, there are important philosophical decisions that a university must make before embarking on any comprehensive commitment to nurturing civic engagement in its students. It must review its basic purpose and mission, decide which values it will privilege, be clear about which democratic philosophy it will embrace and enact, and be willing to accept the consequences of its words and actions. In the spirit of the model advocated here, it makes sense that such philosophical discussions be conducted deliberatively and inclusively. Imposing such decisions from the top would surely undermine both the effectiveness and legitimacy of resulting programs. On some campuses, nurturing those efforts that begin at the grass roots, as service learning did on our campus, can hasten an institution's path to becoming an "engaged" campus (Furco 2006).

Programmatic Considerations

Even when an institution resolves these philosophical matters there is much to consider in implementing an intentional program of civic engagement. Our four-year experience with the Democracy Fellows suggests to us certain prescriptions for implementation. Although a program of this sort is not completely replicable, there are, nevertheless lessons from our experience that we think can be helpful to other institutions as they go about this work.

There are distinct advantages to beginning the work of developing students as citizens through a program, such as the Democracy Fellows, that selects a smaller group from the student body and works closely with that group developing deliberation skills over an extended period of time. There are also certain elements of the program that we think are critical to its success and should be part of any program adopted elsewhere.

Size. Limiting the size of the group reduces the human and monetary resources needed to run the program. With 30 students enrolled in the Democracy Fellows program, we had two faculty members running the program with some administrative help from undergraduate and graduate student assistants. Because we were conducting a research project at the same time, there were teaching load reductions and additional administrative tasks and costs connected with our project (especially in organizing, taping, and transcribing all the interviews and focus groups over the four years), which would not be necessary for a school seeking to replicate it. Because our university already had a first-year seminar program in place, the goals of which fit well with our subject of democracy and deliberation, we were easily able to insert the classroom experience at the start of the program into the schedules of the students and faculty involved. Because of the time commitments expected of the students, we did offer a small scholarship that increased each year they remained in the program.[13]

Intensity. Because we were working with a smaller group of students, we were able to work with them more intensely than might otherwise have been possible. Having agreed at the start of the program to participate in a set number of activities scheduled over the course of the four years, the students scheduled other activities around the Democracy Fellows work and saw it from the start as one of their extracurricular activities rather than an add-on. This allowed us to gradually build their skills over time, starting with the practice of deliberation and framing in the seminar and working up to the organization of the campus and community deliberations. Each level of activity built on the last and their understanding of, and ability to, practice deliberation grew as a result.

Deliberative resource development. Finally, while it could be argued that selecting a smaller group limits the impact of the training, there were important spillover effects from the smaller program that we think are worth noting. With the Democracy Fellows we developed a critical mass of students who were trained in deliberative techniques who could be called upon to use those skills in other settings. When ad hoc situations that called for community deliberation about an issue arose, there was a skill set already in place for making that happen quickly. We found this to be true not only on the campus but in the larger community. We have already noted in reporting the senior-year data that the Democracy Fellows identified all kinds of settings beyond the formal program where they had put their deliberative skills to work successfully—in other campus organizations, in the classroom, and in their personal lives.

---

[13] The stipend was $200 in the first year, $400 in the second, $600 in the third, and $800 in the fourth.

We have talked about the North Carolina Civic Education Consortium, the organization that invited the Democracy Fellows to moderate a forum they held in the area. What a powerful message it sent for the consortium's mission to have young people leading the discussions in an audience made up of high-school teachers and administrators, public officials, and high-school students. During the fall 2004 first-year orientation, the Democracy Fellows played a significant role in a program we presented, entitled "Speaking of Politics. . . ." Rather than choosing a common reading for that year's entering students, the orientation committee asked us to develop a program using the fellows to encourage students to think about the upcoming presidential election and about how to have civil talk about divisive political issues. The Democracy Fellows helped us train approximately 90 juniors, who were serving as student advisors to the new students, in the skills of moderating deliberative talk. During the after-dinner, small-group discussions, which are traditionally focused around a selected text, these advisors led the new students through a deliberative discussion about the election. The feedback from the orientation committee and from faculty advisors who observed the process was overwhelmingly positive. Many said it was the best discussion they had witnessed or participated in during their time as advisors.

Critical elements. It is always important to develop a program that is organic to the institution where it will be implemented, and only the people on that campus know what will work best in that setting. We do not suggest that schools ought to adopt exactly the program that we developed. We do believe, nonetheless, that certain components are critical to the success of any such program.

We will say again that a very strong finding in our work was how much knowledge matters to the ability of students to imagine alternative views of politics and to be motivated to act politically. Presentation of substantive knowledge about deliberative dialogue and the democratic theory that supports and challenges it, early in the program, was important to providing the base for students to assess what they were doing, when it was and was not working, and why. The Democracy Fellows' critical thinking about these topics was well ahead of the class cohort's by the second year and it persisted throughout the study.

It is also essential, in fact perhaps so much so that it goes without saying, that students must have the opportunity to practice the skills of deliberation, and to do so first in safe spaces before going public. In addition to that practice, it is important that there be time for reflection about the practice. We believe that the Democracy Fellows' critical thinking about democracy and deliberation was enhanced by the opportunities to debrief after each of the deliberative experiences they had. This reinforced the classroom learning and heightened their skills with each successive deliberation.

When we look back over the four years and try to identify critical points of learning for the students, there are two particular skills that we think are very important to include in any training for deliberative talk—moderating and issue framing. Moderator training heightens understanding of both the challenges and benefits of deliberation. We presented moderator training as voluntary and about half of the group chose to go through it, giving us a control group of sorts within the study population. What we found is that those who had the training had the most sophisticated understanding of, and appreciation for, the ways in which deliberation can overcome or perpetuate inequalities in political engagement. The heavy responsibility on a moderator for ensuring success in a deliberation helped clarify for them that deliberation can be a valuable means of democratic talk but that it also must be learned —that it is not easy to deliberate without skilled moderation and some understanding of the process. Because moderators in deliberation cannot interject their own views into the discussion, students trained in moderation also showed a greater appreciation for the importance of listening, thinking about the voices that were not represented at the table, and weighing the advantages and costs of policy choices before them.

Framing issues for the two issue books that the students wrote for the campus and community deliberations also had powerful pedagogical outcomes. All of the Democracy Fellows participated in these framings as researchers of the issues and evaluators of the issue book drafts that a smaller group of students wrote. Before each book was drafted, students conducted both archival and interview research on campus and in the community. They were first-year students when they did the research for the campus issue book, and it provided them with substantially more knowledge of the campus and its culture than the average first-year student had. They were second-semester sophomores when they began the research for the community issue book on urban sprawl, and they learned far more about the community within which they lived than many seniors know when they leave. These benefits alone are important. But the framing process also forced them to think about how to take what they had learned through their research and write a book that was about policy choices and the advantages and costs of selecting one choice over the other. They had to discern and articulate the underlying values of each choice and, consequently, to articulate fairly points of view with which they disagreed. The difficult intellectual exercise of discerning how issue choices were coalescing, and then developing the linguistic capacity to word them as unique, discrete, and accurately reflective of public sentiment had great pedagogical pay-off. The contribution to their critical-thinking skills seems clear, but in addition, we believe these framing experiences gave them a sense of connection to and appreciation for the campus and community within which they lived.

Other Opportunities for Integrating Deliberation

While this research shows that sustained exposure of the sort the Democracy Fellows had has considerable impact on knowledge acquisition, skill building, and critical thinking, we also found that short-term exposure to deliberative experiences can have a beneficial effect. Our focus groups with the students who had participated in the campus deliberation but who were not Democracy Fellows demonstrated that students enjoyed the experience, appreciated the opportunity to participate in discussion with diverse voices at the table, and recognized this way of talking as valuable and different from what they had experienced before. Our feedback on the first-year orientation program, while anecdotal, also supports this conclusion.

Clearly, there is great potential for using the deliberative method throughout campus life as a way of modeling civil and productive democratic talk. The potential settings include everything from residence life governance and student organizations, to forums that bridge the town/gown divide. Our "Speaking of Politics . . ." program for the first-year orientation is one example of how and where this might be done. In another project associated with the Kettering Foundation, Miami University of Ohio has begun an extensive program in teaching fraternities how to deliberate about the future of fraternal organizations (Roberts 2004). The project is designed to engage young people in imagining their future and taking responsibility for the organizations to which they are highly committed.

Deliberation offers an effective method of decision making on campus governance issues when the students' voices and input would be important to successful implementation of policy changes related to campus life. In inviting students to deliberate about campus issues, it is important to select issues in which their concerns and conclusions about desirable actions will be taken seriously. A deliberative exercise about a campus issue that makes no use of the outcomes will only breed cynicism about partici-pation rather than a desire to engage. Participation in exercises of this type serve an educative function, but we should be very thoughtful about what we are actually teaching. Students have well-developed hypocrisy sensors, and exercises that create the illusion of democracy without meaningful input to outcomes only discourage future participation (McMillan 2004). If administrators genuinely want student input, or perhaps even better, input from the diverse constituencies of the university, then a well-framed deliberative discussion will produce that, as well as producing a positive democratic experience, which encourages future involve-ment and trust in the outcomes. But if there are decisions to be made where the answer has already been decided by the adminis-tration or where the decision must be made in a particular way, then there is little to be gained and much to be lost by going through a meaningless deliberative exercise.

Deliberation and the classroom. We believe that the deliberative model is one that faculty can adapt to their classrooms well beyond a first-year seminar that focuses on deliberative democracy, such as the one we taught. We presented a workshop for faculty at our campus Teaching and Learning Center on "Using Deliberation in the Classroom," which was well attended and well received. We found that professors are eager to find ways to engage their students in difficult discussions that will not turn into adversarial free-for-alls. They appreciated the ways in which the skills of deliberation could promote critical thinking in their class discussions.

Our data throughout the four years demonstrated that given the time pressures students feel, the best opportunities for engaging students exist in places where they are already committing significant amounts of time. Time in the classroom clearly falls into this category. We found that students are hungry for opportunities for thoughtful and well-moderated discussion of important issues. They had a great appreciation for the classes where this happened, but often found this only in particular disciplines. This suggests that serious thought should be given to how a college might integrate citizenship across the curriculum in the same way that many have integrated other critical skills of writing and speaking.

One caveat is in order, however. While we think our research shows some very positive results from exposing students to the deliberative model of public talk, we believe it is vitally important that exposure to the deliberative model does not lead to unquestioning acceptance of it or, for lack of a better term, to the indoctrination of students. As noted above, not all decisions lend themselves to inclusive deliberation. In addition, we learned through the project, as did the students, that deliberation is difficult and challenging in its own right and that it does not always overcome the problems associated with polarized debate. Sometimes the stakes are just too high for some groups to be willing to seek common ground. Sometimes the skills in oral presentation that advantage some in debate formats carry over to deliberations.

The moderators' skills are extraordinarily important in effective deliberation (a point that merits further research by scholars of deliberation).

Perhaps we were particularly sensitive to this issue because we were attempting to conduct a research project assessing the impact of the program at the same time that we were running the program. Given that reality, we asked continually: What is working? What isn't? We encouraged the students to ask the same questions and they did. In the end, we think our positive findings about critical thinking were, in part, a result of this questioning. We doubt that most people considering the use of the deliberative model will be conducting research as well, but we urge them nonetheless to incorporate this critical view in adopting the model. The process of evaluating what they were doing helped students think through democratic theory and apply the arguments to their own experience. For them it raised issues that are important in being thoughtful citizens, and for us, issues that are important in being thoughtful social scientists: Who is missing from the table? Why aren't they here? What are the barriers to participating in this way? How might they be overcome? When is deliberation an appropriate method of community engagement? When are other actions necessary? Are there flaws in the functioning of the deliberative model that need to be addressed?

Processing study abroad. As we become more aware of our place in the world and as technology links us ever more with that world, it will become increasingly necessary to think about citizenship not just in a domestic context, but in global terms as well. While we did not anticipate it, we found that the experience of studying abroad has a significant impact on students' engagement. This was true regardless of whether students had been in the Democracy Fellows program. One of our Democracy Fellows told us that his overseas experience had expanded his conception of citizenship and forced him to think about what it meant to be a global citizen. Our findings suggest to us that colleges and universities should be thinking about how to encourage more opportunities for overseas travel by their students but also how to structure more opportunities for reflection about their experiences abroad upon their return. For some of the students in both the Democracy Fellows and the cohort, the interviews with us seemed to be the first time they had considered their experience in the context of citizenship and politics, but they had quite valuable insights to share about what they had learned in this context. These data also provided us with further evidence of the importance of knowledge in students' willingness and ability to become involved with politics. Some students returning from overseas realized that their foreign colleagues knew more about American government than they did, and they were embarrassed and challenged by this.

Debriefing study abroad suggests another significant opportunity for encouraging deliberative reflection about democracy and citizenship. Political science, international studies, communication, and other social-science departments could offer post-study-abroad opportunities, either formally for credit, or informally through discussion groups, for students to talk about what they learned from their overseas experience and how that learning shapes their understanding of their own country and citizenship in it.

What the classroom and campus organization settings for deliberation have in common is that they meet students where they are. An ongoing finding in our research is that there are enormous competing pressures on students' time and attention and if a university is serious about civic engagement, simply providing extracurricular opportunities will not be enough to reach that large percentage of the students who are disengaged. Determining how to program civic-engagement learning into the curriculum and student life will have a broader impact than simply allowing political organizations to exist for those who want them.

Our experiment with teaching deliberative democracy taught us far more than we imagined it would. It gave us insights about teaching, student learning, campus life, the state of higher education, and democracy itself. We believe it was a worthwhile exercise that can be adapted by other colleges and universities and can contribute to encouraging a new generation of college students to imagine a different politics than the one they observe and so often abandon. In the end, we believe that higher education has a critical role to play in these efforts, but it is one that should be true to what higher education does best—developing critical minds. Perhaps Thomas Jefferson said it best when he wrote:

> I know of no safe depository of the ultimate powers of the society but the people themselves, and if we think them not enlightened enough to exercise their control with a wholesome discretion, the remedy is not to take it from them, but to inform their discretion by education.

References

Allan, G. 1997. *Rethinking college education*. Lawrence, Kansas: University Press of Kansas.

Andolina, M., K. Jenkins, C. Zukin, and S. Keeter. 2003. Habits from home, lessons from school: Influences on civic engagement. *PS: Political Science and Politics* 36:275-280.

Arnett, R. C., and P. Arneson. 1999. *Dialogic civility in a cynical age: Community, hope, and interpersonal relationships*. Albany: State University of New York Press.

Asen, R. 2004. A discourse theory of citizenship. *Quarterly Journal of Speech* 90(2): 189-211.

Astin, A. W. 1993. *What matters in college: Four critical years revisited*. San Francisco: Jossey-Bass.

Barbaras, J. 2004. How Deliberation Affects Policy Opinions. *The American Political Science Review* 98:687- 701.

Barber, B. R. 1984. *Strong democracy*. Berkeley: University of California Press.

Barber, B.R. 1998. *A Passion for Democracy: American Essays*. Princeton: Princeton University Press.

Barber, B. R. 1999. Deliberation, democracy, and power. *Kettering Review* 31-36.

Barber, B. 2001. Public education and democracy. *Kettering Review* 18-26.

Barber, B., and R. Battistoni. 1993. A season of service: Introducing service learning into the liberal arts curriculum. *PS: Political Science and Politics* 26(2):235-240.

Battistoni, R. 1997. Service learning and democratic citizenship. *Theory into Practice* 36:150-156.

Becker, T. L., and R. A. Cuoto. 1996. *Teaching democracy by being democratic*. Westport, CT: Praeger.

Beebe, S. A., and J. T. Masterson. 2000. *Communicating in small groups: Principles and practices*. 6th ed. New York: Longman.

Bell, D. A. 1999. *Democratic deliberation*. New York: Oxford University Press.

Benhabib, S. E. 1996. *Democracy and difference: Contesting the boundaries of the political*. Princeton: Princeton University Press.

Bennett, S. E. 1997. Why young Americans hate politics, and what we should do about it. *Political Science and Politics* 30:47-53.

Bennett, S., and L. Bennett. 2001. What political scientists should know about the survey of first-year students in 2000. *PS: Political Science and Politics* 34:295-299.

Berelson, B., P. Lazarsfeld, and W. McPhee. 1954. *Voting*. Chicago: University of Chicago Press.

Bohman, J. 1996. *Public deliberation*. Cambridge, MA: The MIT Press.

Bormann, E. G. 1996. *Small group communication: Theory and practice*. 3rd ed. Edina, MN: Burgess Publishing.

Borowiec, J. B., and N.L. Langerock. 2002. Creating empathetic spaces. *Curriculum and Teaching Dialogue* 4(2):79-87.

Boyte, H. C. 1980. *The backyard revolution: Understanding the new citizen movement*. Philadelphia: Temple University Press.

Boyte, H. C. 1989. *Commonwealth: A return to citizen politics*. New York: Free Press.

Boyte, H. C. 1993. Practical politics. In *Education for democracy*. Dubuque, IA: Kendall-Hunt.

Boyte, H. C. 2001. *The civic renewal movement in the U.S.: On silences and civic muscle, or why social capital is a useful but insufficient concept*. Paper presented at the Havens Center, University of Wisconsin-Madison.

Brilhart, J. K. 1995. *Effective group discussion*. 8th ed. Dubuque, IA: Wm. C. Brown.

Bringle, R. E., R. Games, and E. A. Malloy. 1999. *Colleges and universities as citizens*. Boston: Allyn and Bacon.

Bringle, R. G., and J. Hatcher. 2002. Campus-community partnerships: The terms of engagement. *Review of Higher Education* 26:467-486.

Brisbin, R. A., and S. Hunter. 2003. Community leaders' perceptions of university and college efforts to encourage civic engagement. *Review of Higher Education* 26: 467-486.

Burke, K. 1969. *A grammar of motives*. Berkeley: University of California Press.

Burkhalter, S., J. Gastil, and T. Kelshaw. 2002. A conceptual definition and theoretical model of public deliberation in small face-to-face groups. *Communication Theory* 12:398-422.

Button, M. and D. M. Ryfe. 2005. What can we learn from the practice of deliberative democracy? In *The deliberative democracy handbook: Strategies for effective civic engagement in the twenty-first century*, eds. J. Gastil and P. Levine, 20-34. San Francisco: Jossey-Bass Publishers.

Campbell, D. E. 2005. *Voice in the classroom: How an open classroom environment facilitates adolescents' civic development*. CIRCLE working paper, 28. www.civicyouth.org.

Campus Compact. 2002. *The new student politics: The Wingspread statement on civic engagement*. Providence, RI: Campus Compact.

Carey, J. A. 2000. *The engaged discipline*. Paper presented at the Carroll C. Arnold Distinguished Lecture, National Communication Association, Boston, MA.

Center for Information and Research on Civic Learning and Engagement (CIRCLE). 2002. *Youth civic engagement: Basic facts and trends*. The Pew Research Center.

Challenger, D. 2004. The work of "public-making": An interview. *Higher Education Exchange*, 64-75.

Civic Engagement Task Force. 2002. *An engaged university: Renewing the land-grant mission*. Civic Engagement Task Force.

Clymer, A. 2000. College students not drawn to voting or politics, poll shows. *New York Times*, A14.

Colby, A., T. Ehrlich, E. Beaumont, J. Rosner, and J. Stephens. 2000. Higher education and the development of civic responsibility. In *Civic responsibility and higher education*, ed. T. Ehrlich, xxi-xliii. Phoenix, AZ: Oryx Press.

Colby, A., T. Ehrlich, E. Beaumont, and J. Stephens. 2003. *Educating citizens: Preparing America's undergraduates for lives of moral and civic responsibility*. San Francisco: Jossey-Bass.

Constructing civic virtue: A symposium on the state of American citizenship. 2003. Syracuse, NY: Campbell Public Affairs Institute.

Cooper, D. D. 2004. Education for democracy: A conversation in two keys. *Higher Education Exchange*, 30-43.

Cuoto, R. A. 1996. Service learning: Integrating community issues and the curriculum. In *Teaching democracy by being democratic*, eds. T. L. Becker and R. A. Couto, 79-103. Westport, CT: Praeger.

Dahl, R. 1956. *Preface to democratic theory*. Chicago: University of Chicago Press.

Deetz, S. 1999. Multiple stakeholders and social responsibility in the international business context: A critical perspective. In *Organization, communication, and change: Challenges in the next century*, ed. P. Salem, 289-319. Cresskill, NJ: Hampton Press.

Delli Carpini, M. X. 2000. Gen.Com: Youth, civic engagement, and the new information environment. *Political Communication* 17:341-349.

Delli Carpini, M., F. Cook, and L. Jacobs. 2004. Public Deliberation, Discursive Participation, and Citizen Engagement: A Review of the Empirical Literature. *Annual Review of Political Science* 7:315-44.

Delli Carpini, M. X., and S. Keeter. 1996. *What Americans know about politics and why it matters*. New Haven: Yale University Press.

Democracy Fellows. 2002. *Building community at Wake Forest*. Wake Forest University.

Dewey, J. 1960. *Theory of the moral life*. New York: Holt, Rinehart and Winston.

Dionne Jr., E. J. 1991. *Why Americans hate politics*. New York: Simon and Schuster.

Doble, J., I. Peng, T. Frank, and D. Salim. 1999. *The enduring effects of National Issues Forums (NIF) on high school students.* Unpublished manuscript.

Dryzek, J. 2000. *Deliberative democracy and beyond: Liberals, critics, contestations.* New York: Oxford University Press.

Dudley, R. L., and A. R. Gitelson. 2003. Civic education, civic engagement, and youth civic development. *PS Online,* 263-267.

Eisenberg, E. 1984. Ambiguity as strategy in organizational communication. *Communication Monographs* 51:227-242.

Englund, T. 2002. Higher education, democracy and citizenship—The democratic potential of the university? *Studies in Philosophy and Education* 21(4-5):281-287.

Enos, S. L. and M. L. Troppe. 1996. Service learning in the curriculum. In *Service learning in higher education: Concepts and practices,* ed. B. Jacoby, 156-181. San Francisco: Jossey-Bass Publishers.

Enslin, P., S. Pendlebury, and M. Tjiattas. 2001. Deliberative democracy, diversity, and challenges. *Journal of Philosophy of Education* 35:115-130.

Ervin, E. 1997. Encouraging civic participation among first-year writing students. *Rhetoric Review* 15(2):382-399.

Eyler, J., and D. E. Giles. 1999. *Where's the learning in service learning?* San Francisco: Jossey-Bass.

Fineman, H. 2000. Generation Y's first vote. *Newsweek* 136:26-29.

Fishkin, J.S. and R. C. Luskin. 1999. Bringing deliberation to the democratic dialogue: The NIC and beyond. In *The poll with a human face: The National Issues Convention experiment in political communication,* eds. M. McCombs and A. Reynolds, 3-38. Mahwah, NJ: Lawrence Erlbaum.

Flanagan, C. 2003. Developmental roots of political engagement. *PS: Political Science and Politics* 36:635-637.

Fogleman, E. 2001. *Civic engagement: Reviewing the land-grant mission.* University of Minnesota Civic Engagement Task Force.

Freie, J. F. 1997. Democratizing the classroom: The individual learning contract. In *Education for citizenship: Ideas and innovations in political learning,* eds. G. Reeher and J. Cammarano, 153-170. Boston, MA: Rowman and Littlefield.

Furco, A. 2006. *Building the engaged campus: Re-defining community engagement in higher education.* Lecture presented at Wake Forest University, Winston-Salem, NC.

Galston, W. A. 2003. Civic knowledge, and civic engagement: A summary of recent research. In *Constructing civic virtue,* 35-55. Syracuse, NY: Campbell Public Affairs Institute.

Gambetta, D. 1998. *Claro!* Cambridge: Cambridge University Press.

Gamson, Z. F. 2000. Afterword: Defining the civic agenda for higher education. In *Civic responsibility and higher education*, ed. T. Ehrlich. American Council on Education, Oryx Press.

Gastil, J. 2000. Is face-to-face citizen deliberation a luxury or a necessity? *Political Communication* 17:357-361.

Gastil, J., and J. P. Dillard. 1999a. The aims, methods, and effects of deliberative civic education through the National Issues Forums. *Communication Education* 48:179-192.

Gastil, J. and J. P. Dillard. 1999b. Increasing political sophistication through public deliberation. *Political Communication* 16:3-23.

Gibson, C. 2001. *From inspiration to participation: A review of perspectives on youth civic engagement*. New York: Grantmaker Forum on Community and National Services.

Gimpel, J. G., J. C. Lay, and J. E. Schuknecht. 2003. *Cultivating democracy: Civic environments and political socialization in America*. Washington, DC: Brookings Institution Press.

Grant, R. 1996. The ethics of talk: Classroom conversation and democratic politics. *Teachers College Record* 97(3):471-494.

Greider, W. 1992. *Who will tell the people*. New York: Simon and Schuster.

Gutmann, A. 1987. *Democratic education*. Princeton, NJ: Princeton University Press.

Habermas, J. 1984. *The theory of communicative action: Reason and the rationalization of society*. Boston: Beacon Press.

Hahn, C. L. 1998. *Becoming political*. New York: State University of New York Press.

Hale, D. 2001. The natural history of citizenship. In *Friends and citizens*, eds. P. D. Bathery and N. L. Schwartz, 151-170. Oxford: Rowman and Littlefield.

Harriger, K. J., and J. J. McMillan. 2005. Public scholarship and faculty role conflict. *Higher Education Exchange*, 17-23.

The Harwood Group. 1993. *College students talk politics*. Dayton, OH: Kettering Foundation.

Hauser, G. A. 1999. *Vernacular voices: The rhetoric of publics and public spheres*. Columbia: University of South Carolina Press.

Hays, C. 1998. *Alienation, engagement, and the college student*. Lanham, MD: Rowman and Littlefield Publishers.

Hibbing, J.R. and E. Theiss-Morse. 2002. *Stealth democracy: Americans' beliefs about how government should work*. Cambridge: Cambridge University Press.

Higher Education Research Institute. 2004a. *The American freshman: National norms for fall 2004—Political extremes and tech disparities*. Retrieved March 20, 2005, from http://www.gseis.ucla.edu/heri/american_freshman.html.

Higher Education Research Institute. 2004b. *Trends in political attitudes and voting behavior among college freshmen and early career college graduates: What issues could drive this election research report number 1.* Retrieved March 20, 2005, from http://www.gseis.ucla.edu/heri/PDFs/full_political_attitudes.pdf.

Higher Education Research Institute. 2005. *College student survey.* Los Angeles: University of California, Los Angeles.

Hofstede, G. 1980. *Culture's consequences: International differences in work related values.* Beverly Hills, CA: Sage.

Howell, C. L. 2002. Reforming higher education curriculum to emphasize student responsibility. *College Teaching* 50:116-118.

Huckfeldt, R. 1979. Political participation and the neighborhood social context. *American Journal of Political Science* 23:579-592.

Huckfeldt, R., P. A. Beck, R. Dalton, and J. Levine. 1995. Political environments, cohesive social groups, and the communication of public opinion. *American Journal of Political Science* 39:1025-1054.

Ivie, R. L. 1998. Democratic deliberation in a rhetorical republic. *Quarterly Journal of Speech* 84:491-505.

Jacoby, B., ed. 1996. *Service-learning in higher education.* San Francisco: Jossey-Bass.

Janis, I. L. 1989. *Crucial decisions—Leadership in policymaking and crisis management.* New York: Free Press.

Johnson, T., C. E. Hays, and S. P. Hays. 1998. *Engaging the public: An agenda for reform.* Lanham, MD: Rowman and Littlefield Publishers.

Kantrowitz, B., K. Naughton, J. Halpert, and P. Wingert. 2001. Generation 9-11: The kids who grew up with peace and prosperity are facing their defining moment. *Newsweek* 138:46-55.

Kettering Foundation. 1992. *Politics for the twenty-first century: What should be done on campus?* Dayton, OH: Kettering Foundation.

Kettering Foundation. 2001. *Framing issues for public deliberation.* Dayton, OH: Kettering Foundation.

Lange, N. 2002. How did September 11th affect college students? *About Campus* 7(2):21-23.

Lauer, J. M. 1994. Persuasive writing on public issues. In *Composition in context: Essays in honor of Donald C. Stewart*, eds. W. R. Winterowd and V. Gillespie, 62-72. Carbondale: Southern Illinois Press.

Levine, A. 2003. The engaged university. *Higher Education Exchange*, 31-41.

Levine, A., and J. S. Cureton. 1998. Student politics: The new localism. *The Review of Higher Education* 21(2):137-150.

Loeb, P. R. 1994. *Generation at the crossroads*. New Brunswick, NJ: Rutgers University Press.

London, S. 2000. *Higher education and public life: Restoring the bond*. Dayton, OH: Kettering Foundation.

Long, S. E. 2002. *The new student politics: The Wingspread statement on student civic engagement*. Providence, RI: Campus Compact.

Lowry, J. W., and W. Strauss. 2001. The millennials come to campus. *About Campus* 6(3):6-12.

Lucas, S. E. 2004. *The art of public speaking*. New York: McGraw-Hill.

Mallory, B. L., and N. L. Thomas. 2003. When the medium is the message: Promoting ethical action through democratic dialogue. *Change: The Magazine of Higher Learning* 35(5):10-17.

Mann, S., and J. J. Patrick. 2000. *Education for civic engagement in democracy*. Bloomington, IN: Educational Resources Information Center.

Mathews, D. 1996. *Politics for people: Finding a responsible public voice*. Urbana and Chicago: University of Illinois.

Mathews, D. 1997. Character for what? Higher education and public life. *The Educational Record* 78(3-4):10-18.

Mathews, D. 1998. What exactly is "the public"? *Higher Education Exchange*, 70-77.

Mathews, D. 1999. *Politics for people: Finding a responsible public voice*. 2nd ed. Urbana and Chicago: University of Illinois.

Mathews, D., and N. McAfee. 2000. *Making choices together: The power of public deliberation*. Dayton, OH: Kettering Foundation.

McDonnell, L., P. M. Timpane, and R. Benjamin. 2000. *Rediscovering the democratic purposes of education*. Lawrence, KS: University Press of Kansas.

McKee, S. 2004. Epiphanies. In *Going public: Academics and public life*, ed. H. C. Boyle, 20-21. Dayton, OH: Kettering Foundation.

McLellan, J. A., and J. Youniss. 1997. What we know about engendering civic identity. *The American Behavioral Scientist* 40(5):620-631.

McLeod, J. M., D. A. Scheufele, P. Moy, E. M. Horowitz, R. L. Holbert, W. Zhang, S. Zubric, and J. Zubric. 1999. Understanding deliberation: The effects of discussion networks on participation in a public forum. *Communication Research* 26:743-774.

McMillan, J. J. 2004. The potential for civic learning in higher education: "Teaching democracy by being democratic." *Southern Communication Journal* 69(3):188-205.

McMillan, J. J., and G. Cheney. 1996. The student as a consumer: The implications and limitations of a metaphor. *Communication Education* 45:1-5.

McMillan, J. J., and M. J. Hyde. 2000. Technological innovation and change: A case study in the formation of organizational conscience. *Quarterly Journal of Speech* 86(1):19-47.

McMillan, J. J., and K. J. Harriger. 2002. College students and deliberation: A benchmark study. *Communication Education* 51(3):237-253.

Melville, K., T. L. Willingham, and J. R. Dedrick. 2005. National Issues Forums: A network of communities promoting public deliberation. In *The deliberative democracy handbook: Strategies for effective civic engagement in the twenty-first century*, eds. J. Gastil and P. Levine, 37-58. San Francisco: Jossey-Bass Publishers.

Mitchell, G. R. 1998. Pedagogical possibilities for argumentative agency in academic debate. *Argumentation and Advocacy* 35:41-61.

Morse, S. W. 1993. The practice of citizenship. *Social Studies*, 164-167.

Morton, K. 1995. The irony of service: Charity, project, and social change in service learning. *Michigan Journal of Community Service Learning* 2:19-32.

Morton, K. 1996. Issues related to integrating service learning into the curriculum. In *Service-learning in higher education: Concepts and practices*, ed. B. Jacoby. San Francisco: Jossey-Bass Publishers.

Mouffe, C. 1999. Deliberative democracy or agnostic pluralism? *Social Research* 66:745-758.

Murphy, T. A. 2004. Deliberative education and civil society: A consideration of ideals and actualities in democracy and communication education. *Communication Education* 53(1):74-91.

Mutz, D. 2006. *Hearing the other side: Deliberative versus participatory democracy.* Cambridge: Cambridge University Press.

National Association of Secretaries of State. 1998. *New millennium project: American youth attitudes on politics, citizenship, government and voting.* Retrieved March 26, 2006, from http://www.nass.org/New%20Mil%20Exec%20Summary.htm.

Neary, L. 2003. Young people and politics [interview]. *Talk of the Nation.* Washington, DC: National Public Radio.

Nie, N., J. Junn, and K. Stehlik-Barry. 1996. *Education and democratic citizenship in America.* Chicago: University of Chicago Press.

Nussbaum, M. 1997. *Cultivating humanity: A classical defense of reform in liberal education.* Cambridge, MA: Harvard University Press.

O'Connell, D. W. 1997. Teaching the art of public deliberation: National Issues Forums on campus. In *Education for citizenship: Ideas and innovations in political learning*, eds. G. Reeher and J. Cammarano, 135-151.

O'Connell, D. W., and R. H. McKenzie. 1995. Teaching the art of public deliberation—National Issues Forums in the classroom. *PS: Political Science and Politics* 28:230-232.

Osborn, M., and S. Osborn. 1991. *Alliance for a better public voice.* Dayton, OH: National Issues Forums Institute.

Ostrander, S. A. 2004. Democracy, civic participation, and the university: A comparative study of civic engagement on five campuses. *Nonprofit and Voluntary Sector Quarterly* 33(1):74-93.

Owen, D. 1997. *Mixed signals: Generation X's attitudes toward the political system.* Lanham, MD: Rowman and Littlefield Publishers.

Pascarella, E. T., and P. T. Terenzini. 2005. *How college affects students: Volume 2, a third decade of research.* San Francisco: Jossey-Bass.

Pateman, C. 1970. *Participation and democratic theory.* Cambridge: Cambridge University Press.

Patrick, J. J. 2000. Introduction to education for civic engagement in democracy. In *Education for civic engagement in democracy*, eds. S. Mann and J. J. Patrick. Bloomington, IN: Educational Resources Information Center.

Patterson, T. E. 2004. *Young voters and the 2004 election.* Retrieved March 20, 2005, from Harvard University, John F. Kennedy School of Government, Joan Shorenstein Center on the Press, Politics, and Public Policy, Vanishing Voter Project Web site: http://www.vanishingvoter.org/Releases/Vanishing_Voter_ Final_Report_2004_Election.pdf.

Pearce, W. B. 1998. On putting social justice in the discipline of communication and putting enriched concepts of communication in social justice research and practice. *Journal of Applied Communication Research* 26:272-278.

Pernal, M. 1977. Has student consumerism gone too far? *College Board Review*, 2-5.

Pew Partnership for Civic Change. 2004. *New directions in civic engagement: University Avenue meets Main Street.* Richmond: University of Richmond.

Pfeffer, J., and G. Salancik. 1974. Organizational decision making as a political process: The case of a university budget. *Administration Science Quarterly* 19:135-151.

Poole, B. L., and M. A. Mueller. 1998. *Alienation and the "soccer mom": A media creation or a new trend in voting behavior?* Lanham, MD: Rowman and Littlefield Publishers.

Popkin, S. I. 1991. *The reasoning voter: Communications and persuasion in presidential campaigns.* Chicago: University of Chicago Press.

Prince, G. S. 2000. A liberal arts perspective. In *Civic responsibility and higher education*, ed. T. Ehrlich, 249-262. Phoenix, AZ: Oryx Press.

Przeworski, A. 1998. *Deliberation and ideological domination*. Cambridge: Cambridge University Press.

Putnam, R. D. 2000. *Bowling alone: The collapse and revival of American community*. New York: Simon and Schuster.

Rawls, J. 1993. *Political liberalism*. New York: Columbia University Press.

Reeher, G., and J. Cammarano. 1997. *Education for citizenship*. Lanham, MD: Rowman and Littlefield Publishers.

Rice, R. E. 1996. *Making a place for the new American scholar*. Washington, DC: American Association of Higher Education.

Riesman, D. 1980. *On higher education: The academic enterprise in an age of rising student consumerism*. San Francisco: Jossey-Bass, Inc.

Rimmerman, C. 1997. *The new citizenship: Unconventional politics, activism, and service*. Boulder, CO: Westview Press.

Rimmerman, C. 2005. *The new citizenship: Unconventional politics, activism, and service*. 3rd ed. Boulder, CO: Westview Press.

Roberts, D., and L. Hayhoe. Empowering students to shape the future of Greek organizations. *Connections* 15:23-25 (Kettering Foundation).

Rooney, M. 2003. Freshmen show rising political awareness and changing social views. *Chronicle of Higher Education*, 35.

Rosenstone, S. J. and J. M. Hansen. 1993. *Mobilization, participation, and democracy in America*. New York: Macmillan.

Rothwell, J. D. 1998. *In mixed company: Small group communication*. 3rd ed. Fort Worth: Harcourt Brace College Publishers.

Ryfe, D. 2005. Does deliberative democracy work? *Annual Review of Political Science* 8:49-71.

Ryfe, D. M. 2006. Narrative and deliberation in small group forums. *Journal of Applied Communication Research* 34(1):72-93.

Samovar, L. A., and R. E. Porter. 1995. *Communication between cultures*. Belmont, CA: Wadsworth.

Sanders, L. 1997. Against deliberation. *Political Theory* 25(3):347-376.

Sartori, G. 1962. *Democratic theory*. Detroit: Wayne State University Press.

Sax, L. J., A. W. Astin. W. S. Korn, and K. M. Mahoney. 2000. *The American freshman: National norms in fall, 2000*. Los Angeles: Higher Education Research Institute, UCLA.

Sax, L. J., A. W. Astin, W. S. Korn, and K. M. Mahoney. 2001. *The American freshman: National norms in fall 2001*. Los Angeles: Higher Education Research Institute, UCLA.

Schauer, F. 1999. *Talking as a decision procedure*. New York: Oxford University Press.

Schoem, D., and S. Hurtado. 2002. *Intergroup dialogue: Deliberation democracy in school, community, and workplace*. Ann Arbor: University of Michigan Press.

Shapiro, I. 1999. *Enough of deliberation*. New York: Oxford University Press.

Sherrod, L., C. Flanagan, and J. Youniss. 2002. Dimensions of citizenship and opportunities for youth development: The what, when, where, and who of citizenship development. *Applied Developmental Science* 6:264-272.

Smith, W. 2003. Higher education, democracy, and the public sphere. *Thought and Action: The NEA Higher Education Journal*, 61-73.

Sproule, J. M. 2002. Oratory, democracy, and the culture of participation. *Rhetoric and Public Affairs* 5(2):301-310.

Stokes, S. C. 1998. *Pathologies of deliberation*. Cambridge: Cambridge University Press.

Sullivan, W. M. 2000. *Higher education and civic deliberation*. Dayton, OH: Kettering Foundation.

Thomas, N. L. 2000. The college and university as citizen. In *Civic responsibility and higher education*, ed. T. Ehrlich, 63-97. Phoenix, AZ: Oryx Press.

Thomas, N. L. 2003. *Community perceptions: What higher education can learn by listening to communities*. Retrieved March 4, 2003, from http://www.svhe.pdx.edu/cep/resources_conf_hud.html.

Verba, S., K. L. Schlozman, and H. Brady. 1995. *Voice and equality: Civic voluntarism in American politics*. Cambridge, MA: Harvard University Press.

Walker, M. 2002. Pedagogy and the politics and purposes of higher education. *Arts and Humanities in Higher Education* 1(1):43-58.

Weeks, E. 2000. The practice of deliberative democracy: Results from four large-scale trials. *Public Administration Review* 60:360-372.

Young, I. M. 1996. *Communication and the other: Beyond deliberative democracy*. Dayton, OH: Kettering Foundation.

Young, I. M. 1997. *Difference as a resource for democratic education*. Cambridge, MA: The MIT Press.

Young, I. M. 2000. *Inclusion and democracy*. Oxford: Oxford University Press.

Young, J. 2004. Students' political awareness hits highest level in a decade. *Chronicle of Higher Education*, 30.

Youniss, J., J. A. McClellan, and M. Yates. 1997. What we know about engineering civic identity. *The American Behavioral Scientist*, 40(5):620-631.

Zarefsky, D. 1993. The postmodern public: Revitalizing commitment to the public forum. *Vital Speeches of the Day* 60:308-314.

Zlotkowski, E. 1996. A new voice at the table? Linking service learning and the academy. *Change* 28(1):20-27.

Zlotkowski, E. 1999. Pedagogy and engagement. In *Colleges and universities as citizens*, eds. R. G. Bringle, R. Games, and E. A. Malloy, 96-120. Boston: Allyn Bacon.

Appendix A

Deliberative Democracy
First-Year Seminar—Fall 2001

Professors' Information:

Professor Katy J. Harriger
Department of Political Science
Phone: 758-5450
E-mail: harriger@wfu.edu

Professor Jill J. McMillan
Department of Communication
Phone: 758-5407
E-mail: mcmillj@wfu.edu

Seminar Description:

American citizens are increasingly alienated from the political process. This attitude is revealed through declining voter turnout, increased cynicism about the motives of politicians, and a greater likelihood that citizens will lack confidence in the ability of government to solve social problems. A growing number of scholars believe that the solution to this troubling trend is to rebuild civil society through a renewed focus on citizen participation in public policy debates. People like Benjamin Barber, Harry Boyte, James Fishkin, and Amy Gutmann argue that we need a "stronger" democracy in which citizens "join in public work and deliberate over conflicting moral claims" about how the government should pursue the public interest.

This seminar is designed to explore this theory of deliberative democracy and to practice the skills involved in such an approach to citizen involvement in politics. Democratic deliberation involves the "consideration of a diversity of perspectives, a habit of listening, and a careful weighing of trade-offs." The imagined outcome of such an exercise is "the discipline to keep an open mind, the willingness to stand in someone else's shoes, the capacity to change, and the ability to make decisions with others" (David Mathews, *Creating More Public Space in Higher Education*, 2).

We will explore this concept through in-class deliberation exercises, online discussion with other students, and research and writing about public policy issues.

Readings:

1. Photocopied readings for which you will be asked to pay the cost of reproduction.

2. *Public Schools: Are They Making the Grade?* (National Issues Forum, 1999).

3. *Racial and Ethnic Tensions: What Should We Do?* (National Issues Forums, 2000).

4. *Politics for the Twenty-First Century: What Should Be Done on Campus?* (Kettering Foundation, 1992).

Course Requirements:

1. ***Writing Portfolio.*** Over the course of the semester you will write five essays of varying lengths about the topics listed below. You will have the opportunity to rewrite each of them if you want to. At the end of the semester, you will turn in all of the essays as part of a portfolio. This portfolio will make up 55 percent of your grade. The essays submitted in the portfolio can be rewrites or the original, if you were satisfied with that work. The essays will include:

   A. Three- to five-page personal reflection on attitudes toward politics and participation (10 percent)

   B. Three issue research papers of approximately five pages for deliberative exercises (45 percent)

2. ***Preparation/Participation in Deliberative Exercises.*** (in-class and online) (35 percent)

   A. During the semester, we will be conducting **in-class** deliberative exercises in which we consider policy options available on issues, including race relations, public education, and the role of the university in preparing students for citizenship. In order to have an informed discussion about these issues you will be expected to do the assigned readings and write an issue paper with additional research prior to the actual deliberations. During the deliberations, we will follow a particular method of discussion that is **not the usual pro/con debate**. Instead, we will engage in an effort to consider all alternatives, weigh the competing values at stake in each option, think about the trade-offs involved in different choices, and search for common ground on the issue. In other words, in addition to learning about the public policy issue, we will be learning a **method** of discussing policy that is different from what most of us experience in political debate.

B. In addition to our own class deliberation on racial and ethnic tensions, we will be joining a number of students from universities around the country online for the same discussion. This will occur in October. You are expected to participate in this discussion as well.

3. *Final Take-Home Essay Exam.* Assesses the prospects for a more deliberative democracy and your role in it. (10 percent)

Attendance Policy:

We expect you to be in class unless you have an illness, family emergency, or are representing the university in some capacity, such as athletics or debate. For the latter kind of absence, we want to be informed ahead of time with a schedule from your coach or advisor.

Course Outline and Assignment Schedule:

All readings should be completed for the class period to which they are assigned.

I. THINKING ABOUT DEMOCRACY AND THE PUBLIC VOICE

Aug. 30:   Introduction to the Course

Sept. 4:   Diagnosing the Problem
           Read: "College Students Talk Politics"

Sept. 6:   Historical Perspective: What Is the Role of the People?
           Read: Federalist #10 and Essay by "Brutus"

Sept. 11: Historical Perspective on the American Experience
Read: Excerpt from Alexis de Toqueville,
Democracy in America

Sept. 13: Changes in American Politics: How Democratic
Are We?
Read: Excerpt from James Fishkin, *The Voice of
the People*

Sept. 13: **PAPER DUE: Attitudes About Politics**

Sept. 18: Debating Deliberative Democracy
Benjamin Barber, "Deliberation, Democracy,
and Power"
Iris Marion Young, "Communication and the Other"
James Bohman, "Deliberative Democracy and
Its Critics"

Sept. 20: Deliberation as a Democratic Skill
Video: *A Public Voice*
Read: David Mathews, "The Power of Choice"

Sept. 25: Contrasting Debate and Deliberation
Read: "Communicating in Groups"
"Deliberation and Debate: Not One
or the Other"
"Some Key Characteristics of Debate … "

Sept 27: Workshop at Library—Learning Research Skills

Oct. 2: Workshop—Learning Deliberative Skills

Oct. 4: Workshop—Learning Deliberative Skills

II. THINKING ABOUT PUBLIC POLICY ISSUES

Oct. 9: Public Schools: Are They Making the Grade?
Panel Discussion **(Note time change: 11:00-12:00)**
Read: Issue book on public education

Oct. 11: **ISSUE PAPER DUE**

Oct. 11, 16, 18: Deliberative Exercise #1: Public Schools

Oct. 23:   Racial and Ethnic Tensions: What Should We Do?
            Video: *Racial and Ethnic Tensions: What Should We Do?*
            Read: Issue book on racial and ethnic tensions

Oct. 25, 30, Nov. 1: Deliberative Exercise #2: Racial and
                      Ethnic Tensions

Oct: 25:   **ISSUE PAPER DUE**

Nov. 6:   Politics for the Twenty-First Century: What Should
            Be Done on Campus?
            Panel Discussion **(Note time change: 11:00-12:00)**
            Read: Issue book on politics for the
                   twenty-first century

Nov. 8, 13, 15: Deliberative Exercise #3: Politics for the
                 Twenty-First Century

Nov. 13:   **ISSUE PAPER DUE**

III. FRAMING ISSUES FOR PUBLIC DISCUSSION

Nov. 20:   Introduction to Issue Framing
            Read: Photocopied issue book: *Alcohol: Controlling
                   the Toxic Spill*

Nov. 22:   **NO CLASS—THANKSGIVING**

Nov. 27, 29, Dec. 4: Issue Framing Workshop
            Read: Excerpts from "Framing Issues for
                   Public Deliberation"

DEC. 4:   **FINAL TAKE-HOME ESSAY ASSIGNED**

IV. RETHINKING DEMOCRATIC POLITICS

Dec. 6:   Imagining a Different Politics
            Read: Excerpts from "College Students Talk Politics"
            and "Seeing the Problems of Politics Anew:
            Redefining the Challenge"

DEC. 10:   **FINAL TAKE-HOME ESSAY DUE**

Appendix B

Issue Framing: A Teaching Outline
Adapted from the Kettering Foundation's
Framing Issues for Public Deliberation

This process requires a moderator and a recorder to list ideas as they are contributed on flip-chart pages posted on walls. A sturdy easel, colored markers, and masking tape or adhesive-backed flip charts are helpful materials to have on hand. The following steps may be used to deconstruct an existing issue book or to initiate a "new" issue, unique to the students-at-hand.

I. Review the characteristics of a frameable issue. An issue appropriate for public deliberation will be:
    - an issue of broad concern within a community.
    - an issue on which choices must be made, but there are no clear or right answers.
    - an issue on which a range of people and groups must act in order for the community to effectively move forward.
    - an issue on which new approaches may help the community to move forward.
    - an issue on which citizens have not had the opportunity to consider different courses of action and their long-term consequences.
    - an issue on which the decision making of officeholders and other leaders needs to be informed by public judgment, as well as by experts' views.

II. Hone in on the problem by listing concerns:
    - When you think about this problem, what worries you?
    - What worries friends and family?
    - Who is not represented here? What would they say?
        * **Red Flags**
            a. Keep stories short.
            b. Don't have the actual deliberation now.

III. Cluster themes—several, maybe six or seven:
- Seek potential approaches to the problem.
- Start by picking one and asking:
  a. What is the deeply held belief or principle that drives this concern?
  b. What really matters to people when we peel back the layers?
  c. What was "eating" the person who said this?
- Scan the flip-chart pages for other concerns that fit.
- Mark all like concerns with the same color.
- Represent that approach on a clean flip-chart page with the color of those concerns.
- Repeat until most themes are identified.
- See whether outlier concerns need to be subsumed or eliminated.
- Look at potential approaches to see whether there is a common thread.
  Try: "The common problem I see is _____."

IV. Represent approaches to the problem; as a plenary group, write a sentence or two that captures how each approach sees the problem.

Break into small groups to consider each approach.

V. Refine the statement of each approach: review the two- or three-sentence description written by the plenary of how your group's particular approach sees the problem. Determine whether you agree with the wording, and if not, suggest how it might be put in language that is more in line with the small group's thinking.

VI. Recognize the tensions. Questions for the group to consider:
- Is this approach distinctive from the others?
- Does this approach persuade for different reasons than do the others?

- Can everyone find some connection with this approach?
- Does this approach tap into underlying values that people hold?

VII. Consider the benefits and drawbacks of each approach.
- List five or six best reasons to approach the problem this way.
- List five or six best reasons not to use this approach.

VIII. List Actions/Trade-Offs.
- What can we do specifically to implement this approach?
- What trade-offs would be required to carry out each action? That is, what costs or risks would have to be acceptable to people in order to adopt this action?
- Who/what might be harmed or disadvantaged by this action?

 * **Red Flags:**
   a. Avoid abstract terms, such as *encourage*, *favor*, or *support*.
   b. Use concrete language: "increase property tax to distribute to" or "require schools to provide day care, health care, counseling."

Katy J. Harriger is a professor of political science at Wake Forest University where she teaches courses on American politics, courts, democracy, and citizenship. Harriger is the editor of Separation of Powers: Commentary and Documents *(Congressional Quarterly Press, 2003) and the author of* The Special Prosecutor in American Politics, *2nd ed. revised (University Press of Kansas, 2000) and* Independent Justice: The Federal  Special Prosecutor in American Politics *(University Press of Kansas, 1992), as well as a number of articles in journals and law reviews. At Wake Forest, Harriger has been the recipient of the Reid Doyle Prize for Excellence in Teaching (1988), the John Reinhardt Distinguished Teaching Award (2002), and the Schoonmaker Award for Community Service (2006). She can be reached by e-mail at harriger@wfu.edu.*

Jill J. McMillan is professor emerita of communication at Wake Forest University. Her teaching and research has focused on numerous aspects of communication and rhetoric in and around organizations and institutions: corporate identity, the strategies and impact of an organization's public messages, communicative dysfunction among organizational members and groups, organizational democracy and decision making, and pedagogy in  higher education. *Her work has appeared in venues, such as* Journal of Higher Education; Presidential Studies Quarterly; Quarterly Journal of Speech; Journal for the Scientific Study of Religion; *and* Management Communication Quarterly. *She can be reached by e-mail at mcmillj@wfu.edu.*